Joys of War

Joys of War

From the Foreign Legion and the SAS, and into Hell with PTSD

John-Paul Jordan

Pen & Sword

MILITARY

AN IMPRINT OF PEN & SWORD BOOKS LTD.
YORKSHIRE – PHILADELPHIA

First published in Great Britain in 2018 by
Pen & Sword Military
An imprint of
Pen & Sword Books Ltd
Yorkshire - Philadelphia

Copyright © John-Paul Jordan, 2018

ISBN 978 1 52674 314 5

The right of John-Paul Jordan to be identified as Author of this work has been
asserted by him in accordance with the Copyright, Designs and Patents Act 1988.

A CIP catalogue record for this book is
available from the British Library.

Printed and bound in England
By TJ International

Pen & Sword Books Ltd incorporates the Imprints of Pen & Sword Books
Archaeology, Atlas, Aviation, Battleground, Discovery, Family History, History,
Maritime, Military, Naval, Politics, Railways, Select, Transport, True Crime, Fiction,
Frontline Books, Leo Cooper, Praetorian Press, Seaforth Publishing, Wharncliffe
and White Owl.

For a complete list of Pen & Sword titles please contact

PEN & SWORD BOOKS LIMITED
47 Church Street, Barnsley, South Yorkshire, S70 2AS, England
E-mail: enquiries@pen-and-sword.co.uk
Website: www.pen-and-sword.co.uk

or

PEN AND SWORD BOOKS
1950 Lawrence Rd, Havertown, PA 19083, USA
E-mail: Uspen-and-sword@casematepublishers.com
Website: www.penandswordbooks.com

Contents

Acknowledgements

How does one acknowledge such a vast array of travel and interconnections with an abundance of people and places? I can start by humbly saying thank you for still being here. Firstly, to the spirit within for never giving up, even when mind and body had lost the fight. To my beautiful children, my guardian angels, Sonny and Ruby. If that picture of you had not been brought to me while I was unconscious, sadly I would have just being another statistic. To Indi and family in the UK and my family in Ireland, thank you for your prayers and help. It wasn't an easy journey, even before illness, having a child/brother/friend and husband with a way of life in war; the sleepless nights and worry.

There are so many others to mention, and I thank all for every part you have played and continue to play. To the kindness of strangers and the patience of friends and family. For this book, my editor Linsey Hague for her support, advice and eye for detail, and for helping me through some of the problematic editorial processes with vision and integrity. Thank you also to Pamela Covey for her editorial prowess in the later stages of completing this book's editing journey.

I am thankful for the guidance and opportunities bestowed upon me from Helen Lewis and the team at *Literally PR*, whose ideas looked at many aspects of the book from different points of view. I am very fortunate to have Helen as my agent, also. To Heather Williams and Tara Moran at Pen and Sword for all their assistance and hard work.

To all those I have met, many of whom have become friends in my journey, and which for various reasons I cannot mention them all. However, you all know who you are and so thank you for your help. I would like to thank Tony Gibson for his support and guidance throughout my recovery, and Kyra Dobson for her generosity of spirit and understanding, inspiring the best of me from the moment I put pen to paper.

To those I have fought and served along side. Thank you for being there in battle and for your courage; it is an honour and a privilege to go into battle together. And to those on the receiving end of the battlefield, thank you also for your conviction to stand and fight; I respect your courage.

To those still in the trenches; do not lose hope. Victory may seem a distant memory, but this is the battle that counts the most. Many of you have not been to war, but that war can be an inner conflict. Your pain, your suffering is no less, neither are your wounds from your own battles. It matters not how war found us, what matters most is how we find peace, and what life we make from our peace.

Last by no means least, I thank the universe for always delivering what I asked for, whether I liked it or not. Enjoy.

Preface

Wow. I can't believe it; this moment is emotional. Thank you for having the insight and instinct to read my story or, to be more accurate, our story. This book is the culmination of an extraordinary journey of every human emotion possible. For quite some time, even in the heat of the madness, in my mind I knew I had something driving me on. Call it destiny, fate, karma, my duty, whatever. I knew my story could and will help other veterans find peace. How do I know this, you may ask? Well, I never listened to the docs, the shrinks, the nurses or any other pen-pushing idiot who had the honour of working me over when I returned from war. Why didn't I listen? Simply because I couldn't identify with them. I felt no connection with their souls. They had not been to war. They had not taken life. They had not watched it ebb from young lads' faces, boys butchered by IEDs (Improvised Explosive Devices). They were speaking from what they had read in a textbook. My friend, we actually live it, breathe it: it runs through our blood on a daily basis. I would not listen to them because they would not listen to me. You know that feeling: that frustrated, punching, crying feeling, as though you were the muse for the Edvard Munch painting, *The Scream*. Well, the good news is that you can burn that image now. Finally there's somebody who also knows your story. What we both want and need, and above all else deserve, is peace. Peace, my friend. Peace of mind, peace of body, peace of soul, peace of life. I liken it to waking up again and being glad you're alive. Sounds simple? But stay with me. I don't expect you to be convinced so soon. If I were reading this, I'd say get lost. But first, let me tell you about me. You can be the judge of my credentials for finding a way out of war, and into peace.

Jesus, where the hell do I begin? The circumstances of my upbringing to the path life has taken me may seem irrelevant and yet the dots can only be joined by looking back. I truly believe that I was destined to get to this point. The why is yet to entirely unfold, but time takes time. You too have reached this point for a reason. The fact that you are still standing, still fighting, still breathing tells you that your spirit hasn't given up. What your dream or destiny is only you can discover. I sincerely hope, and I have the utmost faith in you and myself, that what I am writing to you, and what you are reading from me, is not a book but a letter about the wars of life, not just on the physical battlefield but in the battlefield of the mind. Though our individual paths may differ, we share similarities: the ups and downs, the emotions to which life has exposed us as we move through our experiences. For too long we've been prisoners of war in our own minds, unable to see an escape route, bruised and battered, weathered and stormed, unable to peer through the darkness of our cells to see the light that will give us hope, let us escape. Yet, if pursued with faith, belief and courage, victory also remains and is still there for the taking. Were you beaten on the battlefield? Never, my friend. Are we going to be beaten on this battlefield against a system of thought? Never. We can't fight the system but we can replace it with a better system and then the old system becomes obsolete. Okay, so better get yourself comfortable; I don't do anything in half measures.

Chapter One

The Wild West

I was born and raised in Ireland. My childhood was unorthodox but generally good craic. I spent my childhood helping my family on the farm or in the family business. This is where I got my penchant for being a bit of a lunatic. With my living room, or more accurately the back bar 'snug', being a pub I spent most of my time either pulling pints or acting the eejit, with someone chasing me for pulling pranks, stealing sweets or supping alcohol when I shouldn't. I did my first 'session' before I was 10 years old. My father had popped outside to tend some cows. There weren't many customers in and all I had to do was pull a pint and tell him who had it and between them they would sort out the payment. In the '80s (and today) people in Ireland were decent and honest so it wasn't a big deal for kids to be working in pubs or on farms from a young age, especially if it was a family venture or adventure.

Anyway, as I got a little older and wise to the world, my dad used to take me on his bootlegging booze expeditions across the border into the north where whiskey and spirits were much cheaper. It was now the late '80s and the IRA and the British army were always battling it out in some form or another. We were there purely on an economic foray. Our alliance has always been to ourselves and neighbours and having the craic. There we were carrying crates of whiskey across this desolate part of the border to a waiting Cortina, to and fro half the night, with gunfire ringing down the valley further along, echoing all the way to the moon and back. It unnerved me but didn't bother me. My payment for not telling my mother that I had been smuggling whiskey on a school night was a huge shiny new toy tractor. There was the old man, his accomplice from the northern side of the border carrying crates of whiskey and me proudly carrying my newly-acquired silence and toy tractor across no man's land. My main task was to be the lookout as the car was so full there was only space for the driver. Daddy dearest thought that with me being small I wouldn't take up any room so instead of an adult taking up the space of five crates of whiskey, I could lie on top facing the rear window. The driver couldn't see through the stacks to the ceiling of the car so I was the lookout for cops and customs. Cops were the lesser of two evils; you could throw them a case or two to help maintain morale. Customs officers were a bit more anal. No craic at all; must have been toilet-trained at gunpoint. You couldn't talk or bribe your way out with most of them but we lived in hope.

This was the trend for a few years. By the time I was 12 I was driving my old man's car, especially on horse-racing days. There would be him and his friends and as the day went on they achieved a suitable beer intake. I was the runner, going up and down putting on the bets for them. Don't get me wrong, I was taking my cut as I went along. You never see a poor bookie. Then, when they couldn't drive, or more precisely pass the breath test – though it was rare when that surfaced, you would have to have taken a fatality for that instrument to see daylight – I'd be their taxi. On one occasion I vividly remember the local Sergeant Garda (police) having an impromptu checkpoint on the way to our village. I duly stopped and rolled down the window; our family is well-known and liked. Here was I, driving, couldn't see over the steering wheel, used to peer through it. The old man and his cronies were well steaming and in great form. I rolled down the window, looked at him and said we were looking for a good pub and could he give us directions. We all burst out laughing including the sergeant. He grumbled at us to take the car straight home, no pit stops. 'Sound,' said I. I thanked him and duly buggered off on my merry way.

By the time I had reached the age of 15, women's mud-wrestling had reached rural Ireland. It was a visiting show and my first taste of the forbidden fruit, well actually climbing onto the roof to look at it from a skylight with some of my school pals. I was working in the bar that night so got to watch it again. Jesus, was I popular at school for weeks after. Even the local priest was in on the action, sinking pints of Guinness, as I brought a tray full of drinks to waiting tables. I winked at the priest and commented, 'Nice to see you're taking an interest in all your flock father.' He told me to get lost and out of his view. Oh man, was the wild west of Ireland great bloody craic growing up.

After the inevitable marriage breakdown of my parents, mother and kids moved to the next village. I still went back home on weekends. It was different now; wasn't home like before but even with the mayhem it was home. My dad emigrated to London again, while I helped in the pub with other stuff. I did more partying than studying, hence the decline in my results towards the end of high school. I had no interest really; it just didn't appeal to me. I am intelligent but I just couldn't concentrate. The school system seemed to suck the life out of us so rebellion was always on the menu as a daily occurrence. Thankfully I didn't apply myself anyway or I wouldn't have had the travels I did. Within a few weeks of graduating from secondary school I was 18 and bound for the Big Smoke as it is fondly called in the west or London Town to you, my friend.

Chapter Two

Kepi Blanc

I briefly spent time with my father while he was still working in London. Thankfully I walked straight into a job in construction. I started out as a labourer. The building site was the Royal Opera House in Covent Garden, central London. After my dad returned to Eire I spent my weekends partying like any other lad who had just turned 19. Young, free and mainly skint by Monday, I was only working to pay for the good times. I eventually knuckled down when I got a position with an architectural cladding and stonework company. I was learning a trade and I liked it. I even stopped partying and got back into fitness, taking up amateur boxing in a club in Camden, north London. It would be a valuable tool and training ethos for the future. Someone or somebody was looking over me or, as I say, I have a few invisible friends. They had to look after me in shifts, I was that busy. I'm surprised they didn't look for a pay rise with the big boss over me, or maybe I'm just worth it. I'm still a piss-taking bastard when I put my mind to it.

Then, on 11 September 2001, for some reason I had the day off work. On a 14in TV in a bedsit in Wood Green, a suburb of North London, like millions of people around the globe I watched in shock, disbelief and sadness at the events unfolding live on air. I was speechless. I think I cried at one stage. It moved me. A lot of people were changed that day, me included. I wasn't angry; I just wanted to explore life further. To that end, I booked a ticket to Paris by Eurostar. I went direct to Paris to find out about the French Foreign Legion. I gathered all the information on a day trip and spoke with a recruitment centre. That night I returned to Waterloo Station, London with my head doing overtime putting together the detailed plan for my new adventure.

I started packing the belongings I had accumulated in my four years in London. Anything I didn't want went into a skip. The rest was destined for Ireland. I didn't let anyone back home in on my plan. I decided to tell them I was going to South Africa to work and backpack as I knew there would be no communication for the first four months in the Legion. I spent a week or so at home, saying my goodbyes and so on. I can tell you something for nothing; I've spent most of my life saying goodbyes. In the end, I decided no more goodbyes; it was see you later. The tears were always tough to hide when you're living out of a suitcase and constantly on the move.

I spent one night in London bound for the Gare du Nord in Paris. I had breakfast at one of those bistro café-type places. I couldn't string a sentence together in French; I just pointed at the menu. I made my way on the Paris Metro to Fort de Nogent, the main enlistment and recruitment centre for Paris. The underground trains looked like subterranean minibuses. Fort de Nogent has an old stone archway outside with large gates; quite an imposing sight for a raw recruit or young traveller looking for adventure. I was taken inside. They don't say much. They put you in a room and you wait. The recruitment corporal came in. He took my passport and left again. I waited some more. He then returned, went through my belongings, handed me my basic toiletries, towel and so on, and kept the rest. Still silence. I thought they're playing hard to get. I was hooked like a fish on a line though. I drew bedding from the stores, got a bed in a dorm and waited. More recruits joined me. Nervous eye contact. I asked if anyone spoke English. Negative. This went on for the next few days: wake up at 5.00 am, ablutions, breakfast, cleaning and hurry up and wait.

Eventually we had enough recruits to make the move to Aubagne in southern France. We would be joined by more recruits from various locations in northern France bound by train. We were all in the Legion's green physical training kit. Shaved heads; God, I looked menacing with it. Brilliant, I thought. All those years of falls, scrapes and fights during my school years had left a lot of scars on my scalp, just what I needed to fit in. We arrived in Aubagne and headed straight to the base which is the headquarters of the Legion, 'Quartier Viénot'. Any of our belongings that were not needed – that is, everything – were put into storage. Money, credit cards, phones and so on. A tip for those joining in: hide money, a phone and cards on you or somewhere safe to access after two or three days. They come in handy when you need some manoeuvrability during basic training. In Aubagne they carry out the basic tests to start your career in the Legion. Paper tests assess IQ and literacy in your own language. There are psycho-technical tests and medical tests and then physical tests: runs, push-ups, pull-ups and the rest. It's straightforward enough. Just give it your best effort. Once we passed all this we went through to the 'Gestapo', the legendary Foreign Legion intelligence branch, which checks the background of all recruits from Interpol and other sources. I passed and upon entry we were assigned a different identity. My name became David Jameson. The recruitment sergeant went through a list of Irish surnames and stopped at this one. He must have had a taste for Irish whiskey, especially the one called Jameson. This would stand me in good stead. A lot of the corporals and sergeants loved Irish whiskey – as I would discover later – and made me like it with their drinking shenanigans in the recruits' accommodation block during weekend nights when we were off but without weekend leave.

I spent the next two weeks mainly waiting around and doing mess hall duties with the other recruits. We also visited the Legion retirement home near Aubagne and the vineyard where they make Legion wine. All the older soldiers and those still fit to work still do service. They are of various ages, some broken, some so institutionalized that they will never walk down Civvy Street. All they have is the Legion; it's their family and for a while it was mine. Then I landed at Castelnaudary, 4th Foreign Regiment at the Legion. Not just recruits, but men and officers from all the other regiments attend courses here for promotion duties and operations. It is home to a very mixed representation of the Legion, and the base is so-called after Captain Danjou.

Once we had all our kit and had sufficient numbers to make a platoon strength we were on the backs of military trucks to go to the 'ferme'. Essentially farms in the remote southern French countryside, this is where you find out if you're tough enough for the Legion. It's downright brutal. Violence, physical exhaustion, little food, little sleep, constant cold in the winter and hot as hell in the summer. It was early November 2001 when I had the honour of going through. Funnily enough, some American/Canadian film crew were doing a documentary for the Discovery Channel about the Foreign Legion. They were chronicling the process from start to finish. I'm on it only in the background running. I was interviewed as they wanted English-speakers but they subtitled the French officers who didn't speak English. They must have thought that subtitling an Irishman who spoke English was taking the piss a bit.

Anyway, back to the training; bloody hell, was it hard going. Blokes were getting bussed out left, right and centre with injuries. I loved it and got on well with everyone. Many were deserting. Myself and a Polish lad called Kudick escaped just to visit the nearest village to buy cigarettes and food. We just happened to knock on the door of a former Legionnaire. He didn't grass us up there and then, but he called it in the following morning. Back at the training farm they didn't know who the escapees were so we all got marched out on parade and assumed the usual position: clenched-fist push-up position. Then the screaming started in the attempt to elicit who had gone AWOL the night before. Eventually we owned up, especially as it seemed easier to stand up to answer the questions than lying down avoiding boots. We didn't actually get in any bother. I think they were impressed with our problem-solving ability and the fact that we were fearless. Some of the corporals said well done. Oh, and it wouldn't be the last time I went AWOL in the Legion.

The winter set in: snow and frost, and for many tears. We had training and French speaking lessons every day, seven days a week, washing outside, no hot water or running taps, all old-school. In the Legion you learn to survive with nothing first. Any extras later are a bonus. We did our 50km Kepi Blanc march.

Once you pass this milestone you receive your famous Kepi Blanc (white cap) in a ceremony at the 'ferme'. We were still doing live-fire training with FAMAS, the standard issue 5.56mm assault rifle of the whole French military. After so many recruits had been let go completely from the Legion or with injuries sustained during training or from relentless sadistic corporals beating the shit out of the blokes, they took a shine to me; not a single bloody scratch on yours truly. Being Irish has a lot of benefits in the Legion. The Irish are very well liked in France; there is a long history between the two countries. Once back at Castelnaudary, the routine for the next few months was learning the chants of the Legion. Marching and singing.

Christmas is a big event in the Legion. Even NCOs, officers and so forth must stay on base on Christmas Eve night. There are dinners and parties among the different companies. As we advanced through our training, we received some leniency, usually access to the Legion bar on base on a Saturday evening. Then crates full of beer back to the block.

The corporals on weekend duty would have us lined up in the corridor pissed and then one by one hauled into their room for some form of punishment. I got on all right; they would pour a huge glass of whiskey. A lot of blokes recoiled or showed fear when the bloody big tree-cutting axe was taken out and the corporals would get you to down the whiskey. Most couldn't do it. I had no dramas: straight down the hatch. Even they couldn't believe it. I even had the balls to ask for a refill. Can you see now why I wouldn't be touched? It isn't only Oliver in the Dickens classic who has asked for more, you know. Most of it was frowned upon, but late night at weekends when officers and senior NCOs were at home with their families, single pissed-up corporals rule the roost and it's part of a rite of passage. The number of fights I had with other recruits. You just couldn't back down or show any weakness. Just go, and go big-style, to hell with the consequences. A few weeks after Christmas we were on exercise in the Pyrenees. I had never skied in my life. An Irishman, a shitload of beer, a pair of skis and some steep hills were an almighty combination. I must have introduced myself to half the trees in the Pyrenees going pissed on- and off-piste, so to speak. We got one night's leave all on the march to the nearest village and bar. I just went the whole nine yards, emerging two days later skint and cold. By the time it came to the last few weeks of basic training, I was told I was going to the engineers. I wasn't too bothered as most of us couldn't wait to get out of basic at this stage. I was a ninja with a mop and bucket like all other recruits in every other standing army in the world. Yet I did have one last hooray on the piss when I buggered off out again AWOL until I came back, or was dragged out of the bar. Got a few weeks in the Legion prison for that one.

We all ended up back at Aubagne for our passing-out parade, and then we would go our different ways to various regiments across France for now. I ended up in the 1st Foreign Regiment (*1er Régiment étranger*) of Engineers, based in Laudon, a thirty-minute drive from Avignon in southern France.

It was more of the same brutal training. Soon after leaving Aubagne and joining the engineers, our first week or so comprised assessments of military skills and physical tests. I was, thankfully, one of the fitter ones; however, my French, or more precisely the lack of it, was slowing my progress down. Although I could apply myself quite well, once I knew what had to be done. That initial confusion of trying to figure out orders. Most of us would ask each other until we came to a consensus or we would be enlightened by those giving us the orders, which usually had the opposite effect of enlightenment. I settled into a routine and where I could do well, I did, so at least my language skills would be excused while I worked on them.

After about six weeks of basic engineer training, we had tests to assess how we were getting on. One of the sergeants from the training department had fifteen years' service in the Legion and was originally from Belfast. I took some heart from the fact that he could speak French in his strong Belfast lilt. Something akin to a cross between Gerry Adams and Gérard Depardieu, if they could be crossed. I hadn't a clue what he was saying, but neither did anyone else. I was pleasantly surprised to learn I did well in all the exams. Although it was busy, certain aspects of the engineers were chilled. Firstly, you had to engage your problem-solving abilities to get over obstacles, unlike the infantry where you just use brute force and ignorance to overcome most barriers. We could stand back and assess the situation but, once the assessing had been done, boy did it feel like the infantry though. After that we were seconded to go on an exercise with another unit within our regiment. The exercise was to transport and build a floating bridge/pontoon for men and vehicles to cross a water obstacle.

Obviously, us newcomers were told to shut up and learn, and I soon got stuck in moving parts to whoever was barking the orders and pointing. The main obstacle I found was trying to keep your balance in the boats as we tightened and fixed the bridge into shape and construction, bobbing up and down while hanging over the edge of a small watercraft with a spanner, was engineering at its finest. What I did take away from that exercise was always look busy carrying something, you are less likely to receive orders you don't understand to do something you don't know how to do, yet without getting roared at.

Back in camp though it could be very boring, being just in the gate, we got the privilege of all the crappy jobs. I, like most legionnaires, would unwind in the regiment bar after work, or if we were in the mood in our dorm, a carryout of beer and let the festivities commence, this was generally how most weeks would pass. Drinking and fighting. I was getting bored of the constant bloody cleaning with mop and bucket. Anyone who hasn't experienced Legion life or any military life and is thinking of joining up would be advised to join your own country's army and do basic training and the full three to five years' service before entering something like the Legion. It's difficult not understanding or speaking the language but to be learning soldiering in a tough arena like the Legion is very hard to endure, yet plenty do it.

When we received our first weekend leave from camp, what a palaver getting your weekend pass signed off, around the different departments. You would swear we were going on an exotic trip but it was to the nearest city, which was Avignon. We just migrated what we did at base to outside the walls, so much as usual. We started a weekend of partying. Avignon is an historic city where the popes were seated during the fourteenth century; it has parts of it including the papal palace that are UNESCO World Heritage Sites. As it is sited on the River Rhône, it is a beautiful city to visit but we were only interested in the bars, clubs and women. Just like all the other Legionnaires that travel in from the various bases in the south-east for weekend leave. Most of the weekend was a blur; I did, however, get back to base on time at the end of leave, which was good progress for me and some of the others. Some of us decided to travel to Paris. On the Sunday morning, after an all-nighter on the piss in Paris, I made the impulsive decision to leave. I had no passport or other items, only the clothes on my back and some cash. I sneaked out of France into Amsterdam and spent a few days R&R there. I managed to get a letter from the Irish consulate so I could fly back to Ireland. It looked dodgy as hell but it worked, although Special Branch at Dublin Airport quizzed me for a few hours until letting me go.

I look back at my time in the Legion with fond memories. Another time or if I had been more prepared maybe I would have stayed on, but I wouldn't have got to where I am today without leaving the Legion; still, it served me well. I learned never retreat; never surrender; fight no matter what the odds; fight and die fighting. Ireland was mellow for me. I then went to Portugal and enrolled in a close-protection officer training for high-risk environments course. This would take place in Lisbon and on the coast probably an hour's drive west of the capital. It was summertime in Portugal and one of the first things I noticed while on the final approach to landing at Lisbon International Airport was that the plane literally was feet above the buildings just as we dropped to touch down on the runway. It was a hot muggy evening in the capital when I met with the course instructor and his assistant. The instructor was a solid-built blond-haired South African, a former member of one of the South African counter-terrorism police units. We drove to the accommodation on the outskirts of Lisbon. We chatted and exchanged formalities; it was more a case of gauging me up, usual stuff from the uber alpha male world that is the security industry, be it private or public. Upon arrival at the villa I and the other course attendees said hello and listened in for the late-night brief for the schedule for the next day. Everybody was Portuguese apart from myself, although most had a very good command of English. There would be five of us for the duration; of the four Portuguese lads two were ex-military and two were from the kickboxing/martial arts community, although one looked like he preferred the steroids more than anything. All decent men at the back of it.

The brief was brief; I didn't mind as I was tired, classroom for the next few days firstly. After all the goodbyes, I unpacked and went to sleep; I thought I only had been asleep for about an hour when I was awoken by some chickens making a racket outside my window. Now that daylight had arrived I could see that the villa was part of a farm holding and my new alarm clock with feathers would be a daily occurrence. We were all convened in a big room with several tables pushed together to resemble a planning room. The instructor came into the room; he was not in his more formal mode, being more direct when talking with you to give it a more military feeling and to start to take us outside our comfort zones. This didn't take long for the others as the class would be in English written and spoken word, the pace of the lectures had to incorporate that for most of the students, English was not their first language. This worked well for my note-taking and processing the information better in real time compared with usually jotting notes down as fast as you can to rewrite it better later that evening while studying everything you missed because you were too busy trying to get to the end of the sentence before the power point moved on to the next slide. The course instructor's assistant was Portuguese and had put most of the logistics together for the course; he was also acting as an interpreter during the lectures. This was the routine for the first week or so, although we would occasionally be outside in the farm grounds for practical demonstrations for walking in formation while protecting a client, or the correct procedures for a team getting in and out of vehicles.

The second week, now that is where they really take you out of your comfort zone, we would be travelling west to the coast through one of the National Parks, this part of the course was to disorientate the students including sleep and food deprivation. The main reason for this is for unit cohesiveness. Break us down individually then rebuild us in a more team manner; like all military and police training the removal of self is paramount. The ego does return but it is more unit-shaped, i.e. it wants to be the best in the unit. We on the other hand just wanted to sleep and eat. As the days drew on with less and less sleep and food, we started to turn on each other; those not pulling their weight or costing us time in some exercise the instructor had ordered us to complete would get bollocked by the others. In one exercise we had to move as a group from one point across some hills and waterway to another destination within a twenty-four-hour period; all the while we were supposed to be hunted by the instructors. We had little food or water; we were being broken down to a point where you had to work as a team for survival. As we passed through the forest and paths, I was laying hand-made traps from the trees and branches while booby-trapping other entry/exit points with wire or broken glass, where we could find it, just to slow the hunter team down. When we made it to the waterway to cross it was deep and cold; we tried to salvage some wood and put some form of a flotation device together, if not to lay on top, at least to take our weight so we could hold on to it while we all swam across together. Obviously it came apart when we needed it the most, so we just made a dash for the last 500 metres or so; we were exhausted by now and this was where the fitness, or more precisely the lack of it, showed. I was not that strong a swimmer but I was fit, the steroid-muncher was under the most pressure. He was close to drowning, so unit cohesion did kick in and we all made sure he just hung on to one of the logs while the rest of us dragged and pushed the log and its hanger-on to the shore. When we dragged our sorry selves onto the shore to catch our breath, within minutes we were all shivering; not that it was particularly cold, just that the body was run down with no food or energy to warm itself. As we knew there were only a few kilometres left, we pushed on. Thankfully we made the finish point and were duly given some food and water. I lit a fire to warm ourselves and cook the rations.

All the time we were being enlightened by the instructors as to where and when we were going wrong, instant morale around the campfire so to speak. At least we were gelling like a team; we all hated the instructors equally by this stage. There would be no sleep either, Jesus there was nothing but despair coming out of this South African's mouth, in our eyes. The last exercise consisted of being dropped at the coast in the early morning, which had the added bonus of normal people being there swimming and enjoying the weather. We on the other hand were going through more physical and mental exhaustion generally to the bemusement of the passers-by. We spent most of the day in the sea, playing out an emergency scenario where we had to evacuate a boat before it sank. We were in a circle with arms interlocked treading water, working as one unit so if anyone was tired the others would keep them afloat. As anyone who has been to the Portuguese coast, especially on the Atlantic side, will tell you, even on calm sea days the waves are rather big and the currents are dangerous at times. We were being thrown about and closer to rocks as the swell intensified. Funnily enough I was more bothered that I looked like a shrivelled prune from being in the water so long, priorities eh? Well, there were some fit girls on the beach. We were ordered ashore and it took every ounce of strength just to make it onto the beach, we could just about stand up. As we were asked various questions on the situation we had been in and what could we do better, the instructor informed us that he wanted us back in the water and to try to reach some rocks out in the swell and climb onto them. After some team discussion on the best way to do this, we figured it was too dangerous and we were in no shape to attempt it with the waves etc. Our instructors asked several questions on why we would not attempt the order. He agreed, stating that we were now working as a team with equal input from all, taking into account each of our strengths and weaknesses.

That was the end of the week-long exercises in the wilderness and we were driven back to Lisbon and our waiting beds; I was tired, sunburned and had cuts all over my hands and lower legs, mainly from the rocks and the water. After a few days of more classroom and drills outside on the farm, the final exercise beckoned. We would be taking a client which was the instructor to a lap-dancing club that was owned by one of the kickboxing attendees on the course, sweet, I thought. By the time we arrived at the club, we had been driving in a protective convoy and doing our foot drills as a close-protection team escorting a client; problem was our client was the instructor. He was enjoying the attention from the girls and getting rather pissed, he was a bloody nightmare to handle, wanting to start fights in the club; you couldn't tell if this was for the exercise or if he was a bastard on the piss. I on the other hand got set up, so one of the strippers would try to get me to leave my post for a private lap dance; you know where this is going already. Not only had I to contend with the argumentative client, now the blonde, slim, blue-eyed tease was trying to get me to stand to attention in more ways than one. All the time I was thinking how can I pass the final exercise, get the private lap dance and get a grip of the client. Oh, but when you want to solve a problem it just comes to you: I said to the girl get a friend to do a private lap dance for the instructor, I will have to follow in to the private area as I was playing the role of his close-protection officer so not to look out of sorts I would have the lap dance also while keeping an eye on my client. I figured I would still pass the exercise as I had a great alibi for any questions during the debrief after. Did it work? Did it hell, smart bastard of an instructor decided he wanted to have two girls dance for him, which included the blonde tease. As I was sure she had fallen in love with me by this stage, all I did was watch as my role as his bodyguard. That put a right downer on it straight away; anyway I passed the final exercise and the course, no dancing though. I had a decent debrief and learned a lot of skills to match what I had picked up in my military career so far.

Now my focus upon returning to Ireland was looking for security work. Iraq was kicking off and there was plenty of work going for anyone willing to volunteer in the private security world. I got work with a Kuwait-American company based at Camp Taji, north of Baghdad. It was a difficult task at times due to logistics; our clients did not have the necessary supplies in the country to do what was required. After years of sanctions most of the electric infrastructure was in poor shape; when we would visit electrical installations and plants you could tell most of the place was being held together by hope. All of Iraq was in a state by now. It was the summer of 2004 and Iraq had turned very violent in April of that year. There were car bombs and ambushes on an hourly basis just outside the Green Zone and on the way to Baghdad International Airport. On the military map the road from the airport to the Green Zone was called Route Irish, I shit you not. It was the most dangerous road to travel in the world. Contractors were getting hit hard and so was the military. The stench of burning flesh stuck in your nostrils even when driving at 100 mph plus. It was a suicide run. Don't get me wrong, I was cautious, but it didn't bother me. The engineers we had been tasked to protect and move from various electric and oil infrastructures in Baghdad and the north were shitting themselves. They would not leave base. Their company lost its contract with the Coalition Provisional Authority.

I had made good friends with a South African contingent on the base that was building and servicing all the accommodation for the US army. I stayed with them while looking for more work; the dole queue in a combat zone was a first for me. It didn't take me long to get a new position in a Protection Security Detail (PSD) role based out of the Green Zone. I wasn't there a week and our convoy got it funnily enough right outside Camp Taji. An RPG (rocket-propelled grenade) went straight through the door of my vehicle and out the other side, detonating against a wall. The hole in the door was 2ft from my head. How it didn't turn me into strawberry jam, guardian angel again. We would have sporadic ambushes and gunfights (firefights with insurgents). It was nice to see them dropping after pulling the trigger but more often than not speed is what gets you through ambushes. This was the norm.

Our accommodation was at Saddam Hussein's palace in Central Baghdad. Luscious place. We were combat taxis for a lot of the staff that worked there. There was heavy drinking most nights. I didn't partake all the time but Thursday was seen as the Saturday night of the Middle East as Friday is holy day and nothing gets done, pretty much like every other day. The place was a farce, with taxpayers' money and blood being wasted all over the shop. On this one particular Thursday night I was drinking up at the pool area with some other contractors. I'm not sure if I was pissed or whether someone had slipped something into my drink. People were swimming and jumping off the 30ft diving board. I grabbed someone's bicycle and duly climbed the ladder. Everyone below was shouting and cheering me to get to the top; it ain't half high, I tell you. Only one way down: to huge cheers and applause I jumped with the bike and plummeted into the waiting water below. I swam to the edge and pulled myself out. Next thing the owner of the bike turned up and his bike was at the bottom of Saddam Hussein's pool. He wasn't a happy chappy and wanted me to go get his bike. I said I could barely walk, never mind swim. I duly organized some former force recon contractors. Force recon is the US marine corps Special Forces equivalent. They love fucking water and were jumping in to fetch the bike wanting to impress the civilian women. I think they left me holding their whiskies while they got to the bottom of the pool. I offered the bike's owner a swig as an apology but he had the hump with me. The rest of the night was a blur to say the least. That was around December 2004. I returned to the UK. I wasn't sure about Iraq at that time. It was dirty and dangerous. Money was okay but there was no insurance; nothing if you got injured or worse. I decided more military experience was in order first.

Chapter Three

There is Gold in Them There Hills

I walked straight back into my old stonework job, courtesy of my mentor and friend, Tim. The new site was Ascot Racecourse Grandstand which was being redeveloped. It was 2005. Iraq was still present in the news and there were whisperings for a stronger NATO presence or mission; wow that word, mission. It's just the desensitized drivel handed out: war is war. What about the effect on the ground, the fighting, the destruction, the pain, loss and suffering? All symptoms of war. You can dress it up all you want for the 9 to 5ers watching the evening news but war is war, my friend.

Somehow, even now, I'm not sure how I came to the decision. I think I had bought a book on military fitness some time previously. I was in the process of physical training. Stonework is also a demanding job and requires skill. I knew at 26 I was too old really to join the army full-time at this point. So I decided to look into reservist units and God gave me 21 SAS (Artists Rifles). I did my homework and sought out any information on preparing for selection: what I needed to do to enlist and be eligible for joining. It's the senior Special Forces regiment in the army. During the Second World War there were two units: 1 SAS and 2 SAS. The Special Air Service (SAS) was raised by Colonel David Stirling, but when he was captured by ze Germans, it was headed by an Irishman, Colonel Blair 'Paddy' Mayne, one of the most decorated soldiers in the SAS and military, who should have been awarded a VC for his many actions but the top brass don't like men who fight back. Even to this day, no member of any SAS unit in the UK will accept a VC until a wrong has been put right. I knew I was heading in the right direction; they seemed to love Irish lunatics who loved to fight and I fitted that bill to a tee. I started training in the evenings after an eleven-hour shift on a building site, slowly but surely building momentum.

I enlisted in December 2005. After Christmas the training began before the aptitude section. Aptitude was the hills phase to see whether you had the physical and mental robustness and, just as importantly, the dedication to put in the hours during selection time and the hours outside in your own time. It was two years of working a day job, getting home and running or at the gym for an hour and a half every day, home to bed; every waking moment is geared towards selection. You eat, drink, work and sleep training. Few make it. It tests you to your limit and beyond, but with that you overcome and a new sense of belief is instilled in yourself and your ability to handle any situation. It was deep winter, and January and February was map-reading theory and exercises. You have to prove your ability to navigate through mountainous terrain in Wales with 50lb+ on your back all day, every day. Being Irish I never told a sinner what I was doing. This was for me alone. I quickly got into a routine: 5.00 am wake up and to work. The M25 motorway is a bastard with traffic; it was the only variable in my training regime. It was mostly okay in the morning as I always set off early and work commenced at 7.00 am. You duly missed most of the morning 9 to 5 commuter madness. On the return trip, after an eleven-hour shift, it was a whole different experience. Jesus, I will admit my extensive use of profanities greatly increased sitting in that car park that was called a motorway. I only had a short window in the evenings to get back from Ascot to Hertfordshire, and then short training on my time, generally a 5-mile run followed by one-hour circuits. Then home, where my partner would have dinner waiting, thirty minutes catch-up on the sofa, straight to bed and then lights out for me by 10.30 every night. I was truly blessed with my former wife. I couldn't have done half of it without her support, for which I am eternally grateful.

As the theory training continued unabated I was now in a good routine with work. For anyone thinking of following my path, don't think of the whole thing. Yes, the ultimate target is passing selection but break it up into workable sections. I only planned a week or two ahead. Trained in the day. Just get a routine going. If you want it, if you really want it, like anything in life, it will come to you, but by Christ it won't just be handed to you. You get out what you put in and 100 per cent is what it takes. It's 100 per cent for twenty-four hours and then you sleep, wake up and it's 100 per cent again from when you lift your head off the pillow until that moment when it rests again, and just before you close your eyes you think, yes, I have done all I could do today to further my goal.

The map-reading tests were done and passed. Now it was kit issue; what a palaver that was. Most of it was survival and safety kit; i.e. sleeping bag, poncho, waterproofs, cooking utensils, emergency kit, all the essentials for navigating during night and day and day and night in remote mountainous terrain. You practically had a small house on your back and, mark my words, there were times when it felt like a skyscraper was strapped to it when going up some vertical climb while literally walking round in circles in Wales. It was now March and we were on to guided marches. First a minibus to Brecon during a Friday evening/night. Rock up at some checkpoint in the mountains and bivouac up until morning. Silence and sleep for three hours or so. After working and training all week it wouldn't take long for sleep deprivation to kick in if you let it. Up at 05:00. Scoff, which comprised a boil-in-the-bag on a hexi stove (my favourite was corned beef hash: rocket fuel). Some moron mixed his up and ended up taking chicken tikka masala at 5.00 am in the Welsh wilderness. I pity the poor bugger behind him while his arse cheeks were squeaking under pressure later on that day going up Jacob's Ladder towards Pen y Fan. It's bad enough sucking in air like you're about to have a heart attack but getting the distinctive aroma of curry farts on top I'm sure does wonders for morale. The guided walks were the warm-up and also the directing staff's way of getting to see us apply the theory in practice and starting to assess the lads. You're assessed every second during selection. The directing staff do it, but more importantly, you do it to yourself; it's the blokes who do it constructively and apply it that succeed.

Nevertheless, injuries take some good men out too, without warning. Many are called but few are chosen. The pace of these marches and orienteering exercises was brisk but not what is expected later on. You're just getting the feel for the hills; it's beautiful but no time for selfies here. If you're thinking about getting a photo, that's your female intuition telling you to piss off and join the Women's Institute instead. The directing staff were okay with me. I kept as quiet as I normally do which is not very but, sod it, what you see is what you get. The guided section went on for about six weeks or so. In April the weather in Wales is, well, it's the shits. The weather comes in so fast from the Irish Sea it rises into the mountains and the clag, fog or mist, call it what you like. I called it getting lost in soup and you had to be on the ball with your navigation. To know exactly where you were on the map, the distance and bearing to the next checkpoint, you would read it and visualize the ground: a block of woods, a river or stream, a steep climb and so on. These are the physical markers on the ground that tell you where you are. If all else fails, follow the man in front. You'll be going either the right way or the wrong way; just hope he ain't lost like you. I've seen blokes do this very thing, and then another and another, and within ten to fifteen minutes you see this trail of Bergens (rucksacks) with the orange marker panel on their backs, maybe six lads spaced out about 200 to 400 metres apart. When there was a break in the clag they'd be making good speed in completely the wrong direction. I'd be climbing up a hill while they would be going downhill, never to be seen on selection again. Switch on or switch off, your choice.

Now we were all on our own forced marches across the Brecon Beacons. Typically we were carrying 45lb weight, not including food and water. Early morning set off and march all day non-stop. When finished, bivouac up. Rations and sleep. Injured recruits would make a sorrowful line to the medic station. I never went. I never had injuries, only slight discomfort from having no feet left; nothing that popping painkillers like goddam Smarties couldn't keep me going. Grit your teeth and march on. Faster, always faster. Funnily enough I should have taken this as a warning, but I'm phenomenally fast going downhill. I could literally sprint 2 to 3 kilometres down the mountain like a goat, feet barely touching the ground. Blokes who were only inches away from voluntarily withdrawing (VW) do this and 'Fucking never come back' was roared at you. Those poor souls thought I was mad, a man possessed descending the mountain like Moses with his stone tablet, except in this case it was an Irishman running like an obsessive lunatic to the next checkpoint, roaring 'Get the fuck out of my way.' I wouldn't have been able to stop if I tried; all or nothing, all or nothing. Jesus, those Smarties were a godsend at times.

We were all waiting now for the fan dance. This is the Special Forces equivalent to the standard army 35lb, 8 miles in 1 hour 40 minutes on mainly flat terrain. The SAS demands, commands and respects: 45lb not including food and water, rifle, 24km (15 miles) straight to the top of Pen y Fan, the highest mountain in the Brecon Beacons National Park. Down the other side for an eternity of blistered feet, at a rate of knots enough to make most men faint thinking about it to turn about and do it all over again in the other direction, back screaming, calves tearing, thighs ripping, lungs busting, teeth gritting, mouth foaming, rifle darting left to right in your numb arms. Hips swaying in the same movement, sucking in oxygen like Hillary on Everest. Bloody hell ya. Reach the top of Pen y Fan again. Stop at the checkpoint tent. A two-man tent held down on a windswept creaky rock-strewn mountain top on hope alone. I rocked up with my usual Irish charm and got asked for a joke. Give 'em a cracker. We all laughed. Then I got told to piss off and hurry up. I was on the downward part of the fan dance, heading off the fan like a rocket going to the moon. I nearly missed the turn to cut down the side of Pen y Fan, heading for the Storey Arms. The tourists were coming to meet us but every man for himself on this one; you hadn't enough breath in your lungs to breathe and talk at the same time. Fortune favours the brave. By Christ the damn day-trippers were jumping out of my way. I didn't budge; I was nearly at full sprint with my weight and the house on my back. If I had hit any of them in their puffer jackets and with their walking sticks, Jesus they wouldn't be getting up for a week. I caught up with the top climbers on the way down, passed every bugger, couldn't stop in time for the turnstile beside the finish line, bulldozed into and passed the fan with a few new fans for my determination. I can't take all the credit; when gravity works with you it's amazing. After that we got a little respect; that is, we had two cars of beer back in Sennybridge Camp in the evening. That was it. The fan dance is only a tick in the box for SF soldiers. Do it when you're badged, tick it off and then go on the piss. Well, you have to enjoy tea and medals after every battle.

Then the selection process stepped up another notch. Obviously the distances were increasing as well as the lack of sleep, and the summer heat was now a big factor. The next crucial march was mini-endurance. This was nearly 40 miles. England was in Euro 2006 and were playing Portugal that day but more importantly I made the schoolboy error of going commando because of the heat; thought it would keep the boys cool under pressure. I go commando a lot but not in the field or ops, you don't want chafing setting in. I only learned this lesson the hard way. We set off at 2.00 am first in pairs until sunrise about 4.50 am. I let one guy off. He was too eager to go fast up the hills and I said carry on. About one hour later I passed him and never saw him again. I had a plan and a pace and I was going to stick to it, unlike my army fatigues which were slowly but surely seesawing up and down between my cheeks; pardon the details but one must be accurate in matters of fact. I didn't notice it; too busy marching and watching blokes piling in. I disciplined my water rations. Kept going, passing blokes until I was in third position after having set off way back of the field. The two in front were racing snakes. One never made it into 21 SAS; the other never made it into battle.

Anyway I was about three-quarters of the way round. It was around early afternoon, and it was hot now. I took water on at the last road rendezvous before heading up to the hills again. I was melting at this stage but I stayed smart, kept covered up and wore the camouflage hat, drank most of the water, even added Dioralyte to replace all the missing electrolytes. There was a stream; I knew it was the last water before the other side of the fan some 15km away. I purposefully finished all the water I had left so I could refill the bottles. I took out my water purification tablets, filled my water bottles from the stream and squared away my kit. It's all about doing the basics to a high standard; everything else follows.

On my weekend off I would get in the car at 3.00 am, drive all the way to Brecon from Hertfordshire every other weekend and do the next march in civvys and lightweight backpack and recce the route in slow time. It paid dividends. Quite simply if you want it you will do whatever it takes to get it. I'd then get back in the car and drive all the way home that night. Jesus, this part of the story is taking as long as the march. So I hit the Jacob's Ladder and so did the chafing; it was starting to make an impression on me. I went to the RV tent to give my location, even giving my next grid location, and off I went downhill all the way to Brecon Reservoir. I could see the guy who was in second but too far ahead to catch. This was endurance marching. I picked up the speed, just because it was starting to really hurt and I wanted it to stop sooner than later so get there quicker to sort that out. I landed at the finish line on the road beside the HQ RV; it was the officer commanding selection, big tall man, friendly enough, gave my details. He asked how I was after the 40 mile march. I replied, 'Fucked.' Parked right beside this truck was an ice cream van. I went over and got myself an ice cream and found out that England had lost on penalties again. By this stage I was walking like an elephant bull had screwed me; the chafing between my legs was of epic proportions. I went off and got my head down. Most were still out that evening, some finding themselves in every endearment of that term.

It was almost August and it would soon be test week. Potential recruits from 21, 22 and 23 SAS as well as SF Signals Regiment and Special Reconnaissance Regiment all come together but in separate billeting and on different routes in and around the Brecon Beacons and Elan Valley. The first two or three days are a nightmare only because the queue for the cookhouse is huge; you have to be on the ball with your administration and the like to maximize your rest and sleep. I cannot emphasize enough how important that is; neither will the blokes in the beds next to you if you're a kit molester at 12 o'clock at night trying to perfect something you should have been all over before you even crossed the Severn Estuary into Wales. You carry the Bergen; the Bergen doesn't carry you.

Test week comprised forced marches between checkpoints at top speed; that's as the crow flies. So out on the ground you're going best effort at all times. Miss the cut-off time in one march and you're on your one and only warning. If the yellow mark beside your name is accompanied by another yellow, you just inherited a lot of down time to think about it. I smashed every one though, like all the lads wanting it. Now it was the final march, the Long Drag or Endurance: 40 miles over the Brecon Beacons with 59lb, not including food, water and rifle, and twenty hours to do it. We had finished the previous march on the same day. Get back. Get three hours if you're lucky with the noise of flapping recruits. Up the cookhouse at about 10.00 pm. On to 4-tonners to Talybont Reservoir in Brecon for the near-vertical start. You're well screwed before you start. Most lads can't lift the weight as it's topping 70lb all in. Throughout the week we'd lost weight and strength. Most blokes rolled the pack on the ground and stood up with it strapped to them.

It was nearly midnight now, pitch black but cool in the summer night. You couldn't see anyone; all you could hear was the occasional directing staff telling blokes to turn off their head torches. We're all lined up ready to be briefed by the chief instructor: 'I don't want to see a procession of head torches going up the mountain, switch them off and switch yourself on. Pep talk done.' I waited for my turn to give my details to the directing staff at the starting-point, opened the gate and ascended. Oh, I had done this route during training in the daytime. I knew it was a bitch throughout. Anyway, one foot in front of the other. I joined the steady stream of men with backs bent forward to adjust their centre of gravity. Legs weakened and were burning with the shock-load of the ascent. Hungry heart would see you through, round the first bit of woods. Away from the start point looked up and all I could see was a procession of head torches heading to the clouds above. Sweet, I thought, and switched mine on.

All I can say is that the march from Talybont Reservoir to the first checkpoint at the Storey Arms is what tests you. Either the darkness gets you or you get injured. That's it. Make it past the Storey Arms and into daylight and you're in with a chance, only a chance though. Blokes were going round in pairs or small groups;

someone to egg you on and for you to do the same for them later on. By the time you're halfway you're running on faith alone. The heat was starting to take effect and the body was weakened. It's the ultimate march after months of training to get to here: keep going, just keep going. At any road junction you could see men lying in their sleeping bags, giving in to exhaustion and voluntarily withdrawing. I didn't pay attention; I kept going. I was more interested in the fact that I thought I had a school of piranhas in each boot as that was what it felt like. Even the painkillers the medics were handing out weren't working. Aggression was called for. I kicked a rock which rattled the piranhas in my boots and said 'Any fucking more out of you lot and there will be more of that.' I would give myself more pain to prove the constant typical pain was tolerable. A funny kind of remedy but I'm a funny kinda guy. Oh, I was on a home stretch; only 8 miles to go. I could smell the finish line now. Boy was I psyched out or up, depending on how you viewed it. Picked up the pace as we were slowly coming out of the hills but the ground was getting stony and rocky. It felt like I was walking over hot coals by this point. Blokes were tiptoeing down the path; they could hear me grunting and frothing in the distance behind them. Closer and louder, the swearing was now audible. I was motoring on, swearing in pain. This one lad looked round in disbelief to see me charging through the hot coals. 'You okay mate?' He barely had the energy to form a sentence. I couldn't speak, just roared with aggression and determination to finish this fucking march and go on the piss. I was as thirsty as hell.

I could see the checkpoint ahead. It was roughly a mile in a direct line. The only issue between me and the checkpoint was a big drop and an even bigger reservoir. It was on the other shore. Jesus, did I want to walk on water like never before. Too much sinning to date to attempt that one. I went the long way: 3 miles of hot asphalt on my feet. The road was level with the water, trees bristling in the late afternoon sun. I could taste the first pint now and there is nothing like the thought of going to the pub to inspire an Irishman to greatness. I sprinted round that route. I'd see a fella in front and that was the target: pass him. Then the next, and the next. That's what drove me round the bend towards the finish line. Crossed that bitch. Gave my details. Went behind a 4-tonner. Took off the Bergen which had felt like it had been surgically attached to me, walked over to the water and sat in it. I couldn't be arsed to get up and go for a piss, so I just pissed there like you do in a swimming pool. The relief from the weight of the march, the months of training and the piss felt like a symphony playing in my mind.

Back into the 4-tonner we waited for it to fill up with more souls. We were shattered but proud. Weary smiles were replaced by sleepy eyes and nodding heads as the 4-tonner made its way back to Sennybridge Camp. In I went; got all my admin done straight away. Lads just went to sleep. I knew I had to get it done now before the inevitable seizing up after sleeping. Everything was done: food in the belly, texted my girlfriend and duly had some cold cans of beer before bedtime. I don't drink now. Even recollecting a drink leaves a bitter taste from where it takes you. I was halfway to joining 21 SAS. Another seven months of even more hardcore training. As I was about to find out, the hills phase is a stroll in the countryside compared with what's next.

We had barely recovered from all that hill time: aching, injuries, smashed feet. Now we started continuation training. This was the soldiering aspect. Special Forces soldiers. It ranged from patrolling, ambushes and reconnaissance to weapon-handling and range work; standard operating procedures or SOPs. These are the cornerstone of all training; they become instinctive so when it's well noisy you perform automatically and I can assure you, it don't half get noisy. The very first stage was an 8-mile Bergen run. The pace was blistering. Weight was 45lb, not including food, water and rifle. Not sure what the time was. Keep up with the directing staff. Jesus, was the pace ferocious. Most blokes were still carrying little niggles from Brecon; you could see all their movements were out of kilter. It didn't slow them down or bother them; they were just not yet streamlined, needed to stretch and heal the tendons and fibres and get back to normal service. I struggled. Even after the hill phase my training was the same. You have to put all the emphasis on speed work. I hadn't but I hung in. To make matters worse I was wearing my mountain military boots; they felt like two lumps of concrete. I switched my training to entirely speed work and adjusted my kit. Within a few weeks I was just above middle of the pack. Another few weeks and I led the pack, always. That's what you do; you check your performance list and study what needs addressing and do it. Put together a study plan and goals. It pays dividends quickly. To boot, I certainly didn't like the sound of the one-way conversation between the directing staff and the back-markers in the rear. Real motivational speeches they were. The training continued unabated. No sleep now. It was part of the routine. God, I used to look forward to going to work on a Monday morning for the rest. I was in Fulham working during the week putting 2-tonne staircases in on chain blocks all day. Wow, was that the easy part.

The live firing started with range work in a military training area in South Wales; always ended up in that part of the world. It was non-stop, highly pressurized. Lads were now being rejected steadily on the grounds of non-suitability. Everything was gearing towards a big live-fire exercise and they would have their inevitable cull. It's not just your soldiering skills that are studied but, as I would when I was in the squadron, they look at the character of the potential recruits. Most men ask one simple question: would I serve on operations with this bloke? If you're in an op in an observation point dug into the ground in a hole 3ft deep by 5ft wide, just enough space for two men lying down with kit and covered by branches and sticks, whatever blends into the local environment, it's this that counts. Where you shit into a plastic bag right beside your mate you may have to hold the bag, wipe his arse; it just depends on the situation. Bag it up and keep the memories with you. When it's that cosy you don't want to be wiping the arse of someone you can't stand. I fondly remember two of us in an op shitting, working and having a right laugh laid down soaking wet through, cold as ice cream, but that's what gets you through: the calibre of the man beside you. The live-fire exercise went swimmingly. I was getting a good rep with the directing staff for being very aggressive on the ranges, fast and controlled, knocking down the targets as we passed through at speed. Another hurdle passed.

It was approaching Christmas 2006; final exercise was in January. That would be the combination of everything from all my own-time training to the regiment's. Make or break. It would be gruelling weights, 100lb plus, out in the field for ages, all the time being watched like a hawk. High pressure. High rewards. All good in the hood. After the exercise was done, I waited in the bitter cold of Brecon outside a dark, dingy room. No fanfare here like other regiments: this was 21 SAS born out of the Second World War, cast and forged by the North African campaign, to Italy, to Normandy; no bullshit, just what it said on the tin. I walked in to find out if I was in. The officer commanding (OC) was standing immediately in the doorway with the chief instructor to his left. Some directing staff spattered about; all were looking at me. Oh, don't you worry, I was looking back; no matter where I am, I'm cool as a cucumber. The OC spoke, going through both phases of selection. How I had performed, areas of strength and so on. He then asked me what I thought about getting an interpreter. I replied, 'Well that's up to you, sir, but I can understand you perfectly well.' They all roared laughing. He smiled and said, 'Congratulations, you made it.'

Once all the lads had received the news, good or bad, those of us who had made it were now just other blokes in the regiment, the same as the directing staff. Oh, we were only going in the door, but we *were* in the door and we had earned our place. All on the piss as usual. Assigned to our different squadrons, over the next few weeks kit was issued and my feet adjusted to this new life of training and so on. The only thing that overshadowed this time was the news about my friend and mentor in stonework, Tim. He and I were working out near Stratford in East London. He wasn't feeling great and it was a new job. We were waiting for materials so were just sitting in the canteen. He didn't look great. I suggested he go to the doctor or something. He said he would just go home and have a rest and to call him in the morning. He got a taxi and left his van. I asked him again if he was okay; he said he was. That man was a real gentleman, covered for me and showed me everything he knew about the trade. You could set your watch by him, on time every day and never left a minute early. He helped in his own way without knowing what I was doing in the military. He walked into his house, asked his wife for a glass of water and went upstairs to rest. He died of a massive heart attack within ten minutes of getting home. When I found out later that day, I was lost.

The night of training would have to wait. I was only a twenty-minute walk from the barracks when I got the call. I walked aimlessly around Central London. Jesus, I wasn't expecting that. We buried him a week or so later and I disappeared from work for three weeks. I couldn't go in; I didn't know what I was doing. Eventually the mourning phase passed. I hooked up with John; he and Tim were mates of old. He was younger than Tim but of the same cloth. I would need his valuable friendship on many occasions in the future. I just didn't realize that, in years to come, at one stage he would be keeping me alive.

Back in the 21 we were always training and making new friends in the regiment. Afghanistan was a daily occurrence on the Intel reports and the news. It was heating up but it was soon to get a damn sight hotter. It was now October 2007. There was a good chance for me to be mobilized into a regular army unit to deploy to the Stan, although I was not going with my 21 SAS squadron and it would not be a Special Forces tasking. Oh, this is what I had dreamed about. I wanted to go to war. I can still picture our squadron sergeant major standing in the doorway of a squadron briefing room when the time came to put the question to me. I was inside shooting the shit with some lads, basically having the craic. He said he didn't need to ask me whether I was going, he already knew the answer. We both laughed. In the typical military career a sergeant major never laughs with the new boys on the block, but this is the SAS; officers and men call each other by their first names. Respect among equals. You are classlessness but not ranklessness. So now I was delighted; that was what I wanted. Now I was going to get it with gusto.

Chapter Four

Welcome to Afghanistan

I was buzzing with the news of getting deployed, especially as I was barely in the door. It was only a few weeks into the New Year in 2008. The unit I was joining would be taking over from those that had already been working on this task. We would be doing a Relief in Place (RIP) with them. Intel wasn't being fed down the line, but what we could hear on the grapevine was that they were busy and were knocking seven bells out of the Taliban in Musa Qala and surrounding areas of operations. No driving out of the back of pick-up trucks this time, handing the district capital under some negotiated deal back to the Taliban bastards. Though few in number, our brothers were ferocious in making up for it. As they say, it's not the size of the dog in the fight but the size of the fight in the dog. I had my mobilization dates: 17/18 March 2008. The first thing that stood out for me was, Jesus, I was going to be dry on St Patrick's Day. It was just dandy. I was embracing another Irish passion: fighting, to be exact. We were training and getting numbered out for roles within country. So a training matrix would be produced: basically the courses and so forth and the standards that needed to be met for your role within your patrol make-up out on the ground. These would vary from drivers, medics, Intel, languages, gunners, air controllers, mortars and so on. Every conceivable element. We would be a completely self-sufficient unit on the ground. Like all soldiers I was doing my own research on kit and the rest. Although we would be issued kit, some of it was not suitable. It's always nice to tweak it to your own needs, generally to make you more efficient. Carry what you need in little comforts while on patrol in vehicles or taking over platoon houses like solar-powered chargers and so forth. We were expecting nothing so anything on top was a bonus.

I made my way to London. We would be bussed to the mobilization centre, Chilwell Barracks in Nottinghamshire. Everyone was excited. On arrival at Chilwell we would go through what all reservists do. It didn't matter about your cap badge; paperwork doesn't discriminate. We all crowded into a large auditorium to have a seated heads-up on what the craic would be for the next two days; what departments we needed to visit to get our tick in the box, ranging from the medics department to stores department. With hindsight it was a well-run smooth operation. The military loves that kinda simple can't-screw-it-up challenge, but they manage to from time to time. Most of us just made our own arrangements and didn't bother going to the schedule; we knew where to go first, to beat the masses coming through the door behind us. Get the medics and kit issue out as quick as possible. Dentist was easy; the administration side, or J1 in army parle, would end up being the slowest, with wills or other documents, ID discs and so on. Problem was, if you hit any obstacle or delay in one department you were stuck for the day. There were blokes sitting for hours, just waiting to get seen. Some of us would come out of the NAAFI, go over to the department and ask them for change for the pool table just to wind them up. The great thing about wearing a really nice beret is it works a charm with the female staff. Just charm them. They would be ever so helpful. Oh, I milked that for every last drop. Add in the Irish charm on top: win-win. Some of the lads were heading out to Nottingham town centre for a few beers. It was St Patrick's Day, or evening, by this stage. I didn't bother. I had an early night and made sure I was going to be sorted early doors tomorrow.

Our first taste of training was the regular army pre-operational training centre in Kent. Nice trek down the country. It's set up like a factory; you have a week-long programme with lectures in halls and practical demonstrations outside at various stalls in a big open military training area. All the up-to-date tactics being used by whatever enemy force in which theatre as operations are passed from the front line all the way back. It also demonstrates our procedures for overcoming tactics and threats. I can't emphasize how valuable this resource is. Good hard-earned intelligence picked up in war was fed back through the line so the units coming into country to replace those already there were as up to speed as possible. The tri-service may have a few areas that need addressing but when it comes to this preparation and learning lessons, they are all over it. I commend those that pull together the training from the war zone all the way back; no doubt they've saved countless lives and assisted in injuries being arrested as best they could. To be pre-warned is to be pre-armed.

We got our sleeping quarters arranged; there were about twenty lads to a room. Snoring, farting and swearing were the common themes. Some of these places had no windows to open; it was like gas, gas, gas training but we had a proper laugh down there. Only drama is we usually never wear our berets, just our stable belts, and cover that with a smock, that is a camouflage jacket, but you could tell where I was from with the longer-than-usual hair and the never-take-anything-serious kinda attitude to drill or marching. We were just all in one big gang, irrespective of rank, and chatting on first-name terms. There were some green army senior warrant officers among us, mainly regimental sergeant majors. Oh, you could see them little mushroom clouds going off just above their heads but nothing they could do about it; the commanding officer was bang stuck in the middle of us. He was a lieutenant colonel and a decent man who would come have a brew and sit and chat to you, regardless of rank or how long you were in. I would later find out what a good officer he is.

Jesus, we had no leave or weekend leave for another six weeks or so. After Kent we would be heading back to our homeland Brecon Beacons National Park; even in April it's bitterly cold especially when you're doing vehicle patrols around the various training areas in what were essentially military convertibles and as bulletproof as one too. For the next two weeks I couldn't feel my hands, arms or face. I would talk over the patrol radio sounding like an Irishman who'd just got out of the dentist's chair.

I had knuckled down well by now. We had weekend leave, got back up to Wales and a few of us carried on with our leave. The following morning we had a forced march, a quarter of the endurance march with less weight. Now there were attached arms, so we had signallers, medics and Royal Military Police (RMP) as well. Our task in Helmand was to train the police. As we'd learn, you needed a good imagination to stretch that term, but more on that later. Put it like this: you would have a better chance of turning them into astronauts than police officers. With the amount of opium they took, well, they were halfway to the moon already, but I digress.

I had been out all night and didn't make it to the parade square. Telephoned some pals in my patrol, told them my Bergen and so on was all ready; just grab my uniform and boots. Everyone was getting off the 4-tonners when I was getting out of the taxi. Bad timing. I was avoiding all higher-ranking men like the plague. Managed to find my mates quietly, and got out of my civvy clothes into fatigues. Blended in a bit better now. I had only walked out of a lock-in at a pub forty minutes earlier. I was well pissed. Nothing for breakfast except vodka and Red Bull. I could still taste it. My patrol commander and his second in charge were not happy bunnies. I lit a cigarette; normally have a few during a bender. Thankfully that's gone now. My eyes were like piss-holes in the snow. Got to the start point. We were off. I led that march from start to finish; pissed up the vertical climb like a mountain goat. Apparently we were supposed to stay together. That was mostly not to show the difference in fitness levels between us and the attached arms. I was halfway up Jacob's Ladder on the way to the summit of Pen y Fan. I could see my patrol in the rear. I decided to sit down and let them catch up, had some water and a fag by the time my second in charge had arrived; he was fuming I was so far ahead. I wasn't doing myself any favours here, I thought. I still hadn't found out what punishment there was, if any, for being late; although I was on time for the march, just not the parade. When the attached arms arrived, I took one look at them; they were red, out of breath and about to collapse. I lit another cigarette, took a sip of my water and thought sod it, I'm already in bother, might as well let them have it with both barrels. I said to the staff sergeant and the captain, 'State of those. Hey, never mind, you're as fast as your slowest man.' They'd known for the last three months they were joining us. How come no Einstein in our lot or theirs had the foresight to either get them trained up to a higher level of fitness or just send blokes who were up to it? They didn't have to be nearly as fit as us but at least send lads who don't look like they're about to be wheeled into the back of a goddam ambulance every five minutes. Judging by the faces on my patrol commanders I had pushed the boat out way too far. I extinguished the cigarette; it tasted shit anyway. We all started to climb again. I was going as slow as I could and I was still opening up a distance. If I had had the foresight to pack a *Playboy* mag or something I could have entertained myself the whole way round and fuck the consequences. I got a week's sleeping sentry position as punishment for being late.

Here we were in twenty-man rooms in Sennybridge Camp after the day's training. I took my sleeping bag to go and man a telephone in an office that was closed. It was for emergency calls only; there was a cot bed which is a folding army bed 6ft long and 18in wide. It does the trick. The lad at the administration desk that I manned gave me some DVDs to watch. Now here was my punishment. I had to leave the twenty-man room where blokes were snoring, farting, talking and getting up to go for a piss during the night for my own room with a TV and DVDs. I slept straight for nearly eight hours, no piss-taking either. I had landed right on my feet. When I went to the cookhouse in the morning, I obviously told them that it was shit; phone kept ringing, didn't get much sleep. After a couple of days R&R down at the admin desk they cottoned on that it wasn't much of a punishment. I was reunited with the rest of the gang. Oh well, it was good while it lasted.

We spent several weeks around South Wales training. We had a patrol meeting one evening; I was informed I had been chosen to do a basic language course, a Pashto course. Straight after the meeting I went to see the staff sergeant. I explained that most people had trouble understanding me when I was speaking English, so what chance did the Afghans have with me trying to speak Pashto? He agreed instantly, and was even puzzled as to why they had suggested me for a language course. I said I should go for the .50-cal which is the heavy machine-gunners course instead. He agreed. Oh sweet, I thought.

That course was up near Worksop, in the north of England, a week-long classroom course with one day at the firing range. What a machine gun the .50-cal is. Even if the bullet comes within a few inches of you it will kill or at least seriously wound you from the shockwave alone. The noise of the gun is so bloody hot. Jesus. It has a sullen roar if you're at the business end of it; if it's an anti-aircraft machine gun you would know you were in a serious firefight. After we passed the course, we had the weekend off and it was good to get home. It was getting closer to deployment date so any home time was greatly appreciated. Yet I could sense I was becoming colder towards people. In this line of business emotions are the last things you need or show.

We had another field exercise, again with live firing at the end. This was near Thetford, in Norfolk. It was a green army-run exercise where you take over what can only be described as something akin to the old forts in the cowboy movies with the wooden walls where the wooden posts come to a point at the top all the way around. I got pulled up by one of the directing staff for being too aggressive on the machine gun. It was a smaller one, the general-purpose machine gun. The scenario was that my position was manning a sentry lookout and we come under attack. The guy beside me, a Royal Military Police counterpart, was picked as the injured party for the exercise.

The directing staff overlooking our performance asked me to assist him. I said there would be more casualties if I stopped returning fire. I just looked at the bloke playing injured on the deck and roared at him where was he injured? He said he had been shot in the leg. I replied, 'That's okay, you've got two hands free. Self-help. I'm busy on the machine gun.' Just for the record, that's the correct response; you must look at the bigger picture. You can't be flapping every time someone gets shot otherwise you wouldn't advance or you would be overrun pretty quickly. After the exercise was all done and dusted we were sent back down to Kent to do an updated course of one we had attended in March. The tactics and threat were ever-changing. The course went okay. The only thing that was left on the administration side was to write the goodbye letters. These are letters you write to your loved ones with the mindset that you're dead. Real boost for morale. I did mine pissed and didn't take much notice of them to be honest. I felt then, as I do now, that if you think a certain way you'll invite that into your life. It always seemed to be the blokes who were wary or had it in their head that they would get hit that got hit. A lot of units take blokes out of theatre if their head is too messed up or if they're separated from the main group and put them on duties in the rear of the ops but still in-country. All our crew were just gagging for it. It was late May-early June and we were about to deploy when the news filtered through about three deaths in an IED incident that happened to the unit we were replacing; it rammed home the seriousness of it all. I'm recollecting now and, as far as I remember, I listened to the news but didn't ponder on it; it went straight out the other ear. No disrespect to anyone intended but it wasn't the time to dwell on it. We had weekend leave and then it was back to our locations for the coach to Brize Norton and on to Afghanistan on Monday morning.

Most of us were staying the Sunday night in the barracks. It was a 5.00 am kick-off on Monday. Load kit onto coaches and go. All the military kit was already in-country on the advanced party. We were the main party. I took that statement literally. That Sunday evening a group of us went for a few drinks. I marched back in at 4.45 am with fifteen minutes to spare. Heading to Afghanistan with a hangover, lovely. The Brize Norton departure lounge was full, mainly with people coming back from R&R plus our lot. I had shades on all day there. We boarded a DC-10 with the seats facing backwards compared to a civilian airliner. In the case of an emergency landing you would sink into the seat; it makes more sense than sitting with your head between your knees and praying like it's going out of fashion. I don't know how long the flight was; I was asleep for most of it and rehydrating for the remainder. We landed in Kandahar around 3.00 am. As soon as the doors opened you got the blast of heat, though it smelled a lot better than Baghdad. Then it was into the RAF reception area for more waiting to get a C-130 Hercules down to Camp Bastion. Even military flight stopovers, waiting for the next connecting flight, feel the same as being stuck in some airport terminal in civilian land – that can't sleep/can't stay awake feeling, like the night of the living dead, and you're a zombie – except every so often we had to take cover in concrete bunkers as the incoming alarm would sound. It got boring after a couple of fake alarms and in the end we couldn't be arsed doing it. More tea vicar. Our chaplain was deployed with us; he wasn't going to the bunker so we thought he must have received some divine inspiration and stayed near him, plus we were having a good laugh at the others around us flapping, especially when the siren would sound when someone was in the plastic portable toilets, thunderboxes we called them. You could hear the shit fly out of them as the siren squealed into action; pants between the legs, trying to pull them up, opening the door and running at the same time. You can't beat good morale at 4 o'clock in the morning. Even the hangover was happy.

The C-130 arrived on the tarmac outside. Finally we could board. The propellers were still rotating and roaring. Helmets and body armour on. The procession of soldiers slowly walking up the ramp. Oh, the noise was horrendous. They hand out earplugs like the trolley-dollies hand out sweets before take-off. The flight time is just over an hour. Daylight beat us to our destination. Down the ramp at Bastion. The heat was now rising; it was the start of June. Even back in 2008 Camp Bastion was huge. They had what could only be described as huge white warehouses with rows of bunk beds, 500 to 700 men. The AC worked well considering the size of the units. It was only 9.00 am but any time you stood outside, away from the AC, it was like you were sucking the air from a hairdryer. It usually took us six weeks to acclimatize fully. Keep hydrated, cover up and go out for short periods into the heat, that's what we did. In the evening we attempted a short run to hasten the acclimatization. Christ, it wasn't pleasant. Just dry, dusty and stinky, and that was just me panting my way around Bastion. We were getting issued ammunition for our personal weapons, grenades and so on, and webbing, the utility belt you wear to keep the magazines for your weapon. All the good stuff you need for combat. The first few days in-country revolved around awareness training, either some PowerPoint lectures or going to the ranges to zero your weapon, aligning the sights to your personal physique. Also, the sight would have been knocked out of position in transit from the UK. That's where I got my first glimpse of the infamous Afghan appearing out of thin air a couple of hundred metres in front of you. We were surrounded by coarse rocky desert, with not a sinner in sight. Next time you'd look there's a guy 500 metres from you, just squatting, looking at us. Afghans can squat for hours in that position; it's like they've got an invisible stool between their legs or no stools at home. They just watch you. It's quite eerie at first, but once you understand their way of life in rural Helmand, it's quite innocent and an intrinsic part of their daily life.

We received many lectures and opportunities to demonstrate the practical applications of the lectures including counter-IED training and medical training. The IED threat was rising and rising fast. Some of the patrols in our unit travelled to Musa Qala to relieve the unit in place. They spent a short time in Musa Qala and returned to Bastion. We were going to be taking on new ground south of Camp Bastion. Now the US Marines were taking over up north; they would eventually take it all. They had the resources and the political will to take the hits and a media obedient enough not to paint the ground truth. The plan was for us to be based out of Lashkar Gah, the provincial capital of Helmand. The base was bang in the middle of town and fairly small. We would only have an HQ element here, with planning ops and logistics being led from either Lashkar Gah or Bastion for supplies. The idea was to carry out reconnaissance on where we would be most effective in our tasking for police mentoring. We were part of Operation HERRICK and to that end we ended up being brigade play toy for a while. Once we got our notice to move by road to Lashkar Gah it was fine; we did a night move on dark light - that is with all white light blacked out - and used night-vision goggles and infrared light to see in the dark. It was slow and quiet. It took ages when you came to a vulnerable point like a junction or culvert, a drain running under the road if there was tarmac. Usually, places that had had IEDs detonated in the past had been marked up for checking en route. Got there. No dramas anyway.

The tented accommodation was okay but the AC was non-existent. Whatever fans there were only distributed the hot air evenly throughout the tent. So we were all melting at the same rate. To make matters worse, our tent was pitched right beside HQ tent. If there's one thing true of any organization, unless you're *part* of the command structure, you want to be as *far* away from it as possible; it was more commonly known as the bullshit centre. No matter whether it's a factory, a charity or the military, the closer to where the reaction is, the further you are from the action. Still, I'm a firm believer in making the best of any situation so I used my ingenuity to liberate the AC that was keeping the hot heads cool and moved it into our tent; it was bliss while it lasted but we got booted out of that tent within a week. Apparently we were having too much fun and they couldn't think for the laughter. You need laughter more than any other emotion in a war zone, the ability not to take you or the situation too seriously. Yes, by all means your duty must be impeccable, but do it with a smile or at least don't let it get you down. We were here for a few short weeks, mounting patrols that would last up to a few days out in the field. A few sporadic firefights here and there, but there was nothing meaty as of yet.

Then it was decided that we would start launching patrols in Marjah in southern Nad-e Ali district. No NATO forces had been here in three years; it was the poppy capital of Helmand. In the '50s, the then US government, under the guise of US aid, started building a dam and irrigation channels, man-made tributaries of the River Helmand. The Kajaki Dam was quite a feat at the time, given the logistics, but then they didn't have a huge insurgent threat. Anyway, the work essentially transformed parts of Helmand, especially Nad-e Ali and Marjah into lush tropical green zones, fertile ground for planting seed, be it wheat, poppy, for opium, or fanaticism at the end of a gun. It was beautiful to walk through acres of cannabis plants, a sodding forest of the stuff. If a fire started in the summer heat we would have been stoned for a month trying to get out of it. The ground was so moisture-laden from the irrigation ducts that it was like walking with suction boots on in the mud. It was exhausting with the weight and heat, but those hash leaves were funny to look at. It sums up the now-reality of southern Helmand; it was another aeon, another bygone age that the West had jumped into, handling the locals from the medieval period with cheap mobiles. Apparently it's good to talk.

Oh, we weren't long out of the Cheech and Chong experience when it kicked off. Rounds left, right and centre. The lush green hedges and trees make it nearly impossible to spot the Taliban. You had to go with the thump and crack, or the crack or whizz, depending on how close the bullets were to you. That's the noise of them passing you and the sound barrier, the crack. The thump is the sound travelling to you from the initial pulling of the trigger and the gunpowder exploding to drive the bullet out of the gun on its merry way to you, but the bullet travels faster than the speed of sound so the supersonic crack reaches you first and then you hear the thump, the sound from the firing position. Draw an imaginary line between the two sounds and you're roughly in the area of where the love is coming from. You then return the love to them. This is basically instinctive shooting, simply to return fire to supress the enemy until you fix them in their position. Sounds easy on paper. Whole other ball game in the real world. It was only a shoot and scoot. Bastards were playing hard to get, the bloody tarts.

A few days later we were tasked to go into Marjah again, this time to rescue the police who were so doped up they didn't know they were in Afghanistan, never mind a very liberal version of the Keystone Cops. We travelled out of Lashkar Gah through the sun-baked dirt tracks with craters from IEDs and neglect; tarmac was only a vision in someone's head in this part of Helmand. You could only do

10 mph in most parts or you would end up severely damaging the vehicles and the occupants. Crash-test dummies got easier rides than this. There was more chance of you getting seasick in the desert than trying to return accurate fire from the near-pendulum effect of the axles. All the way we were meeting minibuses packed with women, children and the elderly. Some had mattresses atop the vehicles. All civilians, with frightened looks on their faces. There was I, smiling, willingly going in the opposite direction. Some regular army unit had set up a muster point just outside the Green Zone going into Marjah. It was 3km to the police building, an old fort made of 2ft-thick mud walls. Solid as rock, though imposing, almost medieval in its features. Still we were 3km away on roads that were wide enough for one vehicle and little else. Not many places to turn around. Once you were committed, you were committed. No turning back. It would be a bloodbath as vehicles came to a halt, just one big target. We advanced with the police we had picked up at the training facility in Lashkar Gah. They were shitting themselves and were about as easy to control as herding cats around a field. Every which way but the right way. Oh, you needed the patience of a saint.

We rolled on, kept the police in check as best we could. We got in about 1km. Bang, it was noisy big style. They were hitting us from multiple positions on a parallel path 200 metres from us. Just ducking between compounds and going on foot. RPGs were roaring over us and exploding. Bullets whizzing past me, ricocheting off the vehicle. The police just froze or drove wildly, aimlessly. Most of our vehicles got stopped by the melee the police had created. I spotted the Taliban as I passed through the road junction. Lads were getting out of vehicles; these were all open-top so no cover really. I stayed on the .50-cal and signalled to the last vehicle entering the killing zone where the enemy was. I was sending an extraordinary rate of fire down as the place was in disarray; half our patrol was tied up trying to get a grip of the police who were supposed to be helping. My sergeant shouted at me that the cops were shooting in another direction to where I was shooting. I roared back over the din of the gunfire that the police were shooting bloody everywhere and told him exactly where the enemy was. It was intense.

Our vehicle had the interpreter with us. When it all kicked off he jumped to where I was standing and curled into the foetal position, with the empty red-hot cartridges of the .50-cal which are 6in long and 0.75in thick. I didn't even notice him, that's how busy I was and how much adrenaline was flowing, never mind the rockets and bullets. I had three of those empty cartridges infused to my neck where they were seared between my body armour and skin, with the scars still there to this day. It wasn't until we got out of the ambush that I prised them out. Never noticed it either; that adrenaline is a mighty tonic for a fight situation. We got order restored with the police and we fired and moved our way further into the Green Zone, 2km of an ambush. By the time we got to the police building a fast jet was on station, a F-15 fighter jet that had been deployed to assist us; it was circling around 1,500ft until it was tasked to fly just above the treetops in a show of force. We quickly dismounted and secured the building while the medics treated the injured. We rounded up the police that wanted to leave with us. Even the opium-smoking dickheads were in the mood for getting out of danger. The Taliban were reorganizing; they knew our only way out was the 2km route for which we had just fought tooth and nail for every inch. We distributed ammo again. I oiled up the .50-cal. That bitch was as wet as a pool party at Hugh Hefner's Playboy mansion and it was about to see even more action. The fast jet din, a show of force, was coming in just at treetop level, with engines at full roar. Lovely if you're a tourist but we needed to make tracks, no time for combat snaps here. It started immediately. The cops did what they did best: nothing. We were a six-vehicle convoy with me in the second from the rear. We went firm and put down fire to suppress the enemy while the first three vehicles rolled at a steady pace forward, maybe 500 metres at most, depending on visibility. Once stopped and returning fire from their position, we would move and then so on and so forth, but it was hectic. All the way the enemy was shooting and firing RPGs from both sides of the road. Occasionally the cops would launch RPGs.

The problem with the RPGs is that they have a backblast, and if you're standing closer than 5 to 10 metres there's a good chance of being fatally injured. Now we had to contend with these clowns popping up every so often, trying not to get taken out by the backblast or by the Taliban. You couldn't make this ambush up. It had every scenario in it. It seemed like an eternity getting out of the other side. At one stage, while we were about to move, I had to reverse back and take shots at 5 metres, that's how close they came to taking out the rear vehicle. They just sneaked in between us. Ballsy bastard. Dead ballsy bastard though. Eventually we got out the other side. The green army unit that was doing the outer cordon was gobsmacked; they couldn't fathom how we'd got in and out alive. They said they'd never seen or heard a firefight like it and they had been in Afghanistan nearly five months. As the rear vehicle rolled up to where we had taken a quick reorganization to sort ourselves out, the rear driver, a Welsh lad, smiled and handed out cigars. I duly took one and said, 'You can't beat a good firefight; it's better than sex.' We all laughed. The private who was nearby thought we were insane. He wasn't far wrong. That cigar was tougher to smoke than the firefight. We got all our ducks in a row and took the injured back for treatment at base in Lashkar Gah. The massive ambush and subsequent destruction of the bazaar or market area in Marjah didn't go down with the political players. So we were going back in a few days with Coco the legendary police chief from Musa Qala. We spent the next few days preparing for the operation. We would leave around 2.00 am and pick up the police. Therein started the trouble. Afghans typically don't do anything at night except party or sleep. We were effectively the most heavily-armed alarm clock in history. Spent two hours goddam trying to muster some form of enthusiasm into this lot. Don't get me wrong, when they're up for it, they're up for it but when it's snoozy time, it's snoozy time.

It was one hour before first light and we were not at the forming-up point, that is the starting-point of the operation and the police were, from what my nose could sense, getting ready by smoking hash. When we came to a standstill the vehicle convoy stretched 1km ahead and 1km behind. I wasn't in my usual patrol. My mate had been seconded to be the officer commanding the operation's driver and me his gunner. Obviously my heroics in the last ambush didn't go unnoticed. I was well chuffed to be asked and as I said to the OC at the time, 'Your combat taxi has arrived.' We were using night-vision goggles. The police had their own chemical stimulants to see what they wanted to see. They could not fathom for the life of them why we should waste perfectly good headlights and flashing lights. One of their commanders got bored or too high and switched on the sirens, flashing lights and the radio. Within milliseconds we had the whole police consideration turning this blacked-out, quiet stealth move towards the Taliban and the entry point into Marjah into an Afghan mobile disco: beeping horns, roaring, smoking opium, the lot. The goddam place was lit up like New Year's Eve in Times Square. I was pissing myself laughing as they would roll by in their Ford Ranger pick-up trucks shouting Taliban; they were out of their heads. Oh, I thought, this is going to be a funny day if not a long one.

We got the order; our cover had been blown: go, go, go. Vehicles picked up speed; it was now the *Wacky Races* with the Keystone Cops leading the way. Ah well, they would find the IEDs better than us. As no one was expecting us, we got into Marjah and took up positions in the police station, the schoolhouse and other key locations. It was quiet as a mouse for the day, just sporadic fighting here and there. We stayed for a few days living out of our day sacks and rations. Task Force Helmand decided that an International Security Assistance Force (ISAF) presence in Marjah was untenable; also, there was a lot of political interference on the Afghan side. People had interests in the opium there and there were poppy fields for as far as the eye could see. That part of Helmand was the opium capital and that kinda money bought or had local and provincial corruption thrown in for good measure. After all the fighting and men getting injured it was abandoned because it didn't look good on someone's desk. It would be nearly two years and more than 15,000 troops later before ISAF had a presence in Marjah. Pity, it was good craic and whoever was fighting us, be it the Taliban or the drug lords, the Taliban got blamed for a lot that was local warlord or criminal activity. They're the bogeymen of Afghanistan. They put up a great fight though and it would have been nice going toe-to-toe against them. I may not like the enemy, but I do respect them.

The soap opera that was the ISAF's Task Force Helmand, or TFH to us, and their stage, Lashkar Gah base, their HQ, was a nightmare. Thankfully our HQ had the sense to start to get us out of there entirely as the crack-smoking attitude at the planning meeting for TFH was clear. They were all thinking of medals and their CVs, the old boys' network at its finest, and it showed in the results. What mattered were the headlines at home and the political thought du jour. The ground truth of fighting a war to win while fighting with one hand tied behind your back was not even called into question.

We got tasked to recon into Nad-e Ali, the district just south-west of the base. No ISAF forces in the district capital (DC) either; we were supposed to be doing an eight-hour or so patrol, no more than twenty-four hours was the information at the briefing. Longest twenty-four hours in history if you ask me.

It was a night move-in with our usual stealth, so no mobile disco with us this time. There was a police presence in Nad-e Ali DC at the time. Capabilities unknown. Go in and report on it. The 5 SCOTS (or Balaklava Company of the Royal Regiment of Scotland) were also doing a recce with a platoon strength from the north side; we came from the south. The place erupted with nothing but tracer bullets, those red- or green-coloured light shows you see on the news when reporting from a war zone. Through the night-vision goggles it looked like something out of a *Star Wars* film. Eventually, just before first light, it ceased and we made our way in. There was a construction site for a prison which we took cover in; 5 SCOTS on the other side of the DC occupied a school that hadn't been used for several years. We quickly took up defensive positions and waited at first light for a counter-attack but it was quiet. They'd probably just got their heads down. We assessed the place and the police. Got into a routine. News filtered down that we may be here for forty-eight hours. We had planned for twenty-four but, as for any patrol, all the vehicles had been prepared with supplies to last for a while without resupply if needed. That day we came under attack from 200 metres in front of the prison. This was going to be an hourly exchange. Periodically through the day, starting in the morning, there'd be an attack or counter-attack by us. All quiet for food and snooze. Just before midday, same again. Then settle until four or six. Then, at last light, another attack. They were determined and dedicated.

We'd been there for nearly five days now. A resupply convoy with one of our patrols was tasked with coming into us. They were moving through the night but the Taliban had dug up most of the roads and they were choked into an ambush. It was about 2km from our position to the east. It sounded hot in the killing zone. We were manning a hastily-made sangar (fortification). The HQ element of our patrol was in the main building site manning the radio and so on. So we were not privy to the extent of the ambush, though we knew it was serious and some of us were considering putting together a small team to go out to assist. Sadly orders go down the line not up. So we stayed put, but I knew something had gone wrong. They were too long in the one position which told me huge casualties or they'd broken down or both. You don't stay in a killing zone out of choice. We were itching to get to them now; we had close friends in trouble and wanted to go but we had to hold our position. We just didn't have the manpower. When a small collection finally got the nod to mount their vehicles to go and assist them, it left me on my own in the sangar. I was an expert on the machine guns, so I could hold the position.

By this stage I knew every inch of ground out to my front. I knew where the Taliban firing positions were. I could even make out from where the rockets were being launched. When you get enough incoming you soon learn a lot. It came over the radio that the other patrol had serious casualties. The patrol edged towards the DC, with a quick reaction force of eight men to assist the casualty evacuations; that's all we could spare. It was bare bones holding our position. If the Taliban had known and had carried out a simultaneous attack we would have been close to being overrun. Close, I thought, but no cigar. I was going nowhere. From my position I could see the front vehicle go past. There wasn't a top gunner. I knew the vehicle. It was a good pal of mine. I then heard he had been hit badly. Another four lads had been hit in another vehicle. Arms, legs. Some of the Afghans with them had been killed outright. The MERT helicopter was on its way from Bastion. MERT stands for medical emergency response team. They had a flying hospital, more or less: the best medics, docs doing surgery on board. If you make it to that you've got a great chance of living. However, making it to that is a lot harder in the cold light of day as they pushed into the DC to set up a helicopter landing site and secure it. The Taliban knew we had taken multiple casualties; they knew the Chinook would be coming. Taking out a helicopter is a big scalp for any insurgent. At this stage I was scanning the rooftops to my front some 300 metres away. I could see movement through my binoculars. I radioed it back to HQ; the Taliban had five fighters crawling along to get a good position to hit the helicopter when it arrived. We had an Apache attack helicopter on station but it wasn't at where I was looking, it was scanning where the inbound MERT would be landing and the surrounding area. I radioed in more details. No. I had a chance. I flicked off the safety on the machine gun and started engaging. I put some rate of fire down while radioing to HQ exactly what was going on. The Apache was coming round too. I had tears streaming down my face thinking of my friends waiting for the helicopter; there was no way these bastards were going to stop it. Not while I had breath in my body. They were fucking hammered into the next world. I didn't care if it was heaven or hell they were bound for. RPGs went down. AK-47 rifles fell. Turbans fell. The Apache attack helicopter opened up on them also and confirmed five dead. It felt sweet watching the MERT helicopter zoom off with my mates safely inside. The lad that was in the front vehicle who got hit would later be best man at my wedding.

Once all had settled down there was an eerie silence. It's not a nice feeling after a patrol has taken casualties and you take your body armour off. Take water or a brew of tea; try to make a joke or light of the situation. The comedown of the adrenaline is horrendous. I, like most lads there, was tired. We were staying put. The remainder of the other patrol, with an element of our HQ including our commanding officer, left under the cover of fast jets and Apache helicopter; within a day the Taliban dug up every road round the DC. The siege had begun in earnest. As this was taking place there was a big tick in the box for the brigade, TFH and the politicians in Whitehall: the Kajaki Dam turbine move. This was part of the reconstruction project for the hydroelectric dam at Kajaki in northern Helmand (we were further south). There were no roads, just dirt tracks and desert. Every tour is marked by something that can sell the war to the masses. This time it was the movement of these huge turbines, an incredible feat in itself, but we were doing it in a war zone, taking on the terrain and the natives, the Taliban.

It wouldn't have taken much to take that convoy out. It can be denied whichever and wherever. Money had been exchanged for safe passage; it had to have been, and to be quite brutal it was the best way to get the job done. It was the choice of the cost of the turbines and everything else compared with keeping every warlord, Taliban or whatever quiet for a while until they reached their destination. Intel reports coming through told us that the Taliban had migrated down from those areas to take the DC at Nad-e Ali or stop the ISAF from getting a foothold. Over the next few weeks, hundreds upon hundreds of Taliban kept coming, kept attacking. Some days it would be relentless. We would have Apache on station or fast jets. We were surprised at the assets that we had considering the turbine move was taking place at the same time. With hindsight we were the sacrificial lambs for the Taliban. They had been paid off not to attack the Kajaki Dam move. They also needed their own win for their press releases, just like those in Whitehall. Same shit, different country.

Thirty or so mobilized reservist soldiers and a platoon of 5 SCOTS over the other side held that DC for what would become known as the longest siege since Arnhem, holding out for more than seventy-five days. The statistics I heard about it after the tour were impressive, but they're locked away now. Maybe they will see the light of day. All our supplies were being air-dropped in, first by helicopter and then, when that was too dangerous, parachuted in. I don't know how much weight I lost. Near to 2.5 stone. Sleep was non-existent. Yet was it memorable, was it fun! Yes, the fighting was intense. I was like every other man, fearless, but it's those precious moments when it's quiet, the brews, the laughs; just mates keeping each other going through some brutal war fighting. The weeks dragged by. Word came that half of us were getting pulled out. A late-night helicopter would airlift us out with relief coming in. We didn't want to go. Some officer wanted his glory, I suppose.

Up, up and away. You couldn't see an inch in front of you; the sand blown up by the Chinook was like hot razors hitting your face, eyes closed, even with goggles on. We had bugger all to carry. Remember it was only supposed to have been a twenty-four-hour patrol. Left hand on the shoulder of the man in front. Heads down in the backdraft of the engines. Slowly up the ramps and out. We landed at Lashkar Gah. No proper sleep, food or shower in months. Surrounded by the enemy and plenty of dead enemies may I add. Straight back to bullshit. The cookhouse was open. The chain of command was too scared to say that under army rules any man coming off a patrol has up to six or eight hours to shower, shave and so forth. You're entitled to head straight to the cookhouse, especially if you've been under siege while everyone else is fattened up to the hilt on three square meals a day and NAAFI breaks and protein shakes at the gym. 'Fuck 'em,' I said, and we all walked straight in. No one came near us. We stank to high heaven and cleared the place. Either that or it was the solid look of aggression that had been etched onto our faces from the ceaseless battles that properly told them to leave us alone: they don't look like the kinda blokes you mess with. Problem with getting back onto normal food is the digestive system isn't used to it. The food tasted divine and it ran through us. We got only two or three days before we were sent out on more patrols. It was full on; we were glad to get away but it was the cookhouse we missed. We were back on rations, but we had a big supply. We took over a police checkpoint; this was R&R for us. We carried out some police training and started to put the weight back on and get some regular exercise after the siege. TFH were now planning a huge operation to break the siege. No. 16 Air Assault had left theatre. Now it was some other brigade. Same shit, different day. I never passed any notice; this changed hourly and that was brigade HQ and the crack-smoking officers.

After about one week's R&R on the 601 highway between Lashkar Gah and Geresh we were to close the position: take all supplies and break up the place. I volunteered to drive all the explosives back in a Snatch Land Rover. Owing to the IED threat there was a 500m excursion between my Snatch and the rest of the convoy. I had about half a tonne of explosives and ammunition. It wouldn't have passed any green army regulations in transport, nor that I was chewing cigarettes and had a stowaway wild Afghan dog in the passenger seat keeping me company. That's the only reason I volunteered. So I had peace and quiet. I knew no one would expect me to do anything, sitting on top of a van full of explosives. I had a few flasks of tea, music blaring and the puppy pissing all over the place. Sod it, you need to relax when it's stressful. Got there in one piece anyway, to Lashkar Gah base. It was buzzing with the fresh meat from the changeover at brigade. Everyone wanted to make a name for themselves. We started prepping. I was delighted that our patrol got the honour of going down the middle, straight towards the DC. Coco the police chief and his merry crew were joining us. It had all the elements of a good scrap. It was November by now and five months in with no leave. I was itching to be first to break through. I was on point. First in the patrol, we would be fighting our way through. I had a mini me, a light 5.56mm machine gun. Went through bullets like babies go through nappies. Coco was fearless; didn't give a shit. No weapon; just his pistol. He would be commanding from the front with his walkie-talkie. Afghans don't mess about; they are straight down the middle, toe-to-toe in action. It's reckless but it gets results if you're fast and furious. I loved it. Between us we had more than 500 or so: soldiers, Afghan police and Afghan army. It showed that the training was slowly starting to pay off, but it was very fragile.

It took about a week to break through completely. Sadly we didn't get to go to the prison; we were just east of them on a flank. It was hectic enough. During one break in the fighting my patrol commander and I were chatting beside a police pick-up truck when I noticed what appeared to be a boomerang in the sky 500 metres in front of us. Next thing, bang. The pick-up truck took a direct hit from a Chinese-made 106mm rocket. The Taliban – or local fighters more commonly known as ten-dollar Taliban, those who would be paid to fight, no experience, either bored or in need of money for drugs – launched it out of a wheelbarrow, a goddam wheelbarrow. The police gave chase down the road and caught them. I manned the machine gun until it died down and, fair play, the cops caught them. Coco's crew were on the ball. They were misfits but they knew how to rock 'n' roll at the back of it. The rocket missed me by 5ft. No shrapnel, nothing. Two police officers were injured but my mate Des, the patrol commander and I were just fine. There were some skirmishes here and there but, for the most part, it had died down. Also, winter was setting in fast in the mountain passes between Afghanistan and Pakistan. A lot of the fighters would migrate south through Garmsir and into Pakistan towards Quetta and the Pashtun areas of the tribal belt on the north-west frontier, taking a break until fighting season begins in spring. The local Taliban and Afghan Taliban stay over the winter; it's the foreign fighters who move during winter, returning to their families. I and three other friends of mine were due back in the UK to start the Special Forces briefing course for recruits looking at joining 22 SAS. So we were being pulled out two weeks earlier than the main party. All was done. While waiting on the flanks of the operation we were clock-watching. We knew our flights were leaving within a couple of days and it was the last briefing course.

Before full-time selection started in January there was no time to spare. We would be straight out of Afghanistan going on a briefing course which was a pass or fail course. You had a swimming test that consisted of diving off a 30ft drop. That was easy: just jump and gravity did the rest. There would be a combat fitness test

(CFT), 8 miles with 55lb on your back and we were in a hurry to get there. So I used my initiative and informed command that we had secured a lift with one of the green army units going back from the operation to Lashkar Gah. We liberated a Snatch vehicle and waited for the other unit. After a few hours an Afghan army patrol approached that was heading that way. We piggybacked onto the back of them. No counter-IED procedures. Nothing with this lot. Pedal to the metal. I was driving. Lashkar Gah was coming under rocket and mortar fire from the west and the provincial governor's residence had been attacked. We drove straight through the lot. When you've got a flight to catch, you've got a flight to catch. We made it into Lashkar Gah town centre and towards the base. For the last mile the Snatch was dying; we had to push it the last 800 metres into the base. We arrived at the gate. Some young female private opened the gate; her jaw dropped at the sight of us. Stinky. Mixed dress. I had a jungle green shirt on and desert camouflage trousers, beard and wit to boot. She asked who I was with. I said I was with the Woolwich. I referred to an advertisement for a building society in the UK. In my nice Irish accent I broke the tension; it was funny. We pushed the vehicle into the safety of the base. One of the lads went in to inform command we had made it back. He reported back that they were flapping; the unit we were supposed to be getting a lift with was lost. Sod 'em, we were starving now. Oh, the cookhouse was like heaven again. You can't wait to eat properly when you're salivating in line waiting to be served.

Cleaned ourselves up and got our kit packed; within twenty-four hours we were at Kandahar. It was like another planet compared to where we had been: people in uniform, shops, fast food outlets. This wasn't a war zone; this was a theme park. We got our flights back to the UK and landed at Brize Norton to damp mid-winter in the south-east. It was amazing. Green grass and fields. Blighty never seemed so majestic as that Sunday morning leaving the airport in the hire car.

Within a few days I rocked up to Hereford for the briefing course. It started with checking in at admin and getting your paperwork in order, and then accommodation. I bumped into a few lads from the paras I had met early on tour; they had been back over two months getting fit for the course. I told them I had only been back in-country a few days; it showed too. How I passed the swim test I'll never know. After just short of six months in the desert to then be surrounded by water, wearing your army uniform while swimming, was surreal. The speed march went fine. We had some tests on paper as well. At the end of the week we'd find out if we'd passed or not; it was easy enough to know. I vividly remember the directing staff going through the test and asking at the end whether there was anything else we would like to see up on the PowerPoint about the test. I shouted, 'Yes. The answers.' Always one for the smart comment irrespective of the situation, but it had recently got a lot of us through some tough times. Later I would learn that our unit had clocked up the most hours in combat for TFH and held Nad-e Ali DC in the longest siege since Arnhem. We broke a load of records. Some of my mates got awarded the Military Cross (MC) for their actions in that ambush and we had taken a lot of casualties. All in all, we proved we were worth our weight in gold. It was Christmas. Two weeks and then 22 SAS selection beckoned. No rest for the wicked.

Chapter Five

For the Craic

I had no post-operational tour leave. I remember being at Chilwell Barracks after the tour ended. We were reunited with the rest of the squadron. Demobilization, or demob for short, was basically just the reverse of when we started out. Going around the different departments again: medical, stores, administration and so forth. It was easy and stress-free, apart from the hearing test. My ears were still ringing. They are to this day from gunfire and explosions. I will have constant white noise drumming away because of the hectic battles and lifestyle of the last fifteen years or so. I was in the hearing booth, which is like a phone booth with a seat. It's sound-insulated and you wear a pair of headphones. Different variations of noise – very low at the start and then a little higher – are used to measure your hearing range. I couldn't hear half of it. You have a handle in your hand with a button at the top to press every time you hear the noise. It varies from left to right ear. I just kept pressing the button regardless. The young reservist came in and said that it was coming up on the test what I was doing. I said, 'I can't hear you. Shout louder.' We laughed and then I told him, make me pass the test. I did with flying colours. While I was in the administration department I learned that my post-operational tour leave would be cut short because I was going on 22 selection. I told them that test week started in early February, though I didn't inform them that the build-up phase of the course actually started in early January. So, while the vast majority of troops returning home from Afghanistan were spending time with family, friends and the barstool, I would be doing Special Forces selection all over again, with no break from Afghanistan and straight out of operations. So, into the Brecon Beacons and I loved it, to be home again in those mountains. It was the best place in the world after a tour de force like I had just done. Lush green Welsh wet mountains. Heaven in South Wales, who would have thought, eh? Most of the recruits would have spent at least the last three months, many even way longer, preparing for the hills. My preparation was done in battle and in my mind. That's where you win or lose. Everything starts and finishes in the mind.

I spent Christmastime in Herefordshire and Yorkshire with my fiancée's family. I was eating like a horse just to fatten up. I did a few runs and some light marches, nothing really. Just resting and eating and enjoying peacetime. I knew how it would go anyway. It's just a condensed version of the prolonged 21 SAS selection. Although the two selection courses are very different beasts in some ways, they both test your physical and mental strength and beyond. All I can say is if you're going into it with apprehension or fear, you need to change your mindset: break it down into bite-sized chunks and picture in your mind that you're completing a stage, a mini-goal. Bit by bit it's done. Sounds just dandy on paper but it will make you a man. I drove to Sennybridge Camp. The motor was full of kit for the hills phase: extra food, kettle, home comforts like pillow, blankets and had a sheet of plyboard to go under the mattress. The bunks at that camp are like hammocks; when you lie down on them you're bent like a banana. Not good for your back or recuperation after marching all day. Any soldier can rough it; a good one makes himself comfortable.

Once I had signed in, done all the paperwork and been allocated a bed space in the dorms, I unpacked and stored my valuables in a locked container; it might be Special Forces selection but there are a few undesirables walking about. We got our briefings and found out which directing staff would be taking us on the guided marches for the first week or so when they assess your map-reading ability. I have no idea how many recruits there are to start with; around the 250 mark I suspect, judging by the queue in the cookhouse. It doesn't take too long for the number to start depreciating. The winter months of January-February 2009 were some of the worst in decades. The first week went fine. All the keen-as-mustard would-bes were all hot on the heels of the directing staff. I stayed just off the front pack, not really bothered about the ass-licking. The directing staff can see right through it. More importantly I'm not that kind of bloke. What you see is what you get.

The day started about 4.00 am. It was cold, dark and raining. Well, it's Wales and it was mid-winter. We were waiting in the parade square, sitting on our Bergens, waiting for the 4-tonner, the old Bedford trucks with wooden seats. Special Forces selection gets dispensation from health and safety. These are relics from the 1970s and the conditions were part of the psychological aspect of selection: bone-shaking, wind-strapped and wet. Many a man was broken by these before they'd even reached the start point of the march. Trick was to get on, get warm and get a flask of tea and some food into you. Although you had a big fry-up breakfast, the cookhouse is all you can eat; by the time you have spent an hour to an hour and a half on the 4-tonner, all that food had been burned up just keeping us warm and keeping the mind active and positive. I always got extras in the cookhouse with a flask of tea. I needed it. I was still on Afghan climate control. An Irishman with a tan in Wales looks odd.

We had weekends off which was great. The second week varied between forced marches and physical training, that is, beasting sessions. Beastings is the endearing term for gruelling and punishing physical training, runs up and down hills, push-ups, fireman-carries, stretcher races and so on. Anything to push you to your limit and beyond, physically and mentally. The number of blokes that would instantaneously pick up injuries was a feat to behold. Sometimes you'd wonder whether they actually knew what they'd signed up for. By this stage a few of the directing staff were aware of my presence. That can be a good thing or a bad thing. Firstly, I was 21 and secondly, I was Irish. I tried to keep a low profile and for anyone who has ever met me it's difficult to put those two together with me. There wasn't much I could do about it. I just kept going. It was hard going but I knew I would make it. I felt strong. The weather was deteriorating steadily. I don't know how much food I was eating but I just couldn't get enough into me.

Time was flying by. I had done all this with 21 before. I knew the ground, the routes, the best goat paths to take for speed. I had spent the past couple of months in Afghanistan; I knew nothing could put fear into me.

Week three: one more week and then it would be test week. The intensity of the marches was rising. Recruits were dropping like flies. The queue for the cookhouse was now tolerable. I had made the acquaintance of lots of lads by now, either in the 4-tonner or waiting in the queue. There were a handful of Irish lads, a few Scottish, even fewer Welsh and the rest English, some Aussies, New Zealanders, a few Fijians thrown in for good luck and Gurkhas, the little crazy bastards. The weather was horrendous up in the mountains. Cloud, wind and rain. Visibility was crap. You just had to keep moving or hypothermia would quickly set in. The 4-tonners parked at certain road checkpoints were filling slowly and steadily with volunteers. It's called the Jack Wagon. Poor lost souls, that's what they looked like peering out through their sleeping bags and hooded jackets. Boys trying to be men.

Now the cold snap was starting and the damp was drying up. We were coming to the end of week three. The weather now was serious. It was white-out every morning and no sign of stopping. Some of the marches now were just complete and pass. We hadn't even got to test week. The vehicles the directing staff was using, including the 4-tonners, were getting stuck in the snow. It was bitterly cold. When you're carrying 50lb of weight for several hours up and down mountains at best speed you get a sweat on. The worst time was at a checkpoint, especially if there were two or three waiting to give the details to the directing staff. Chill would set in and will would set out. I didn't fuck about. Wham, bam, thank you ma'am. I was well-known by the directing staff now and usually had to come up with a joke at the tent because they were bored and needed some entertainment, while you're standing outside in anything up to 3ft of snow with half a house on your back at the top of a mountain trying to be a comedian. Thankfully it came naturally to me; they would burst out laughing and then tell me to piss off, I was behind time. Thanks, I thought. I didn't leave camp for the last weekend before test week. The roads were treacherous and I wouldn't risk not making it back or getting stuck on a motorway when the time could be better spent walking around in circles in Wales. Well, my mother always said I would go far.

The Sennybridge camp has poor living accommodation: it's a throwback to the 1980s, with wooden chalets with bed spaces for up to twenty men plus their kit. Toilets, showers and so on are in separate blocks. No real heating system and all wooden doors and windows. Cold and damp. Every day we were trying to wash and dry muddied and soaked uniforms and dry out boots for the following morning. This part of the administration, after and before the marches, is hugely important as your body needs maximum sleep to regenerate and heal. Being quick and diligent at this paid huge dividends as the weeks went by, especially starting and during test week. Sleep was broken at best with so many people in these chalets getting up going to the toilet, snoring and the like. Always get a bed space as far from the door and one of the ends near the wall so nobody is passing you during the night, with the door constantly opening and shutting near you. Keeping your life quietly refined to a decent routine so you have your focus on the next march was of the utmost importance. If you don't do it in the barracks, you won't do it in the field or on operations.

Sunday evening: we were all summoned for the test-week briefing. Wow, the numbers had dwindled substantially. Everybody got a seat, including the mice. I'm listening and taking notes, wrapped up like a boiler in the heating press, big puffer jacket, the best socks in the world. Thick socks or, as I say, tick tocks. Bridgedale mountain socks. Oh, they were just morale for your feet. After you've being marching all day when you get to the finish line you could be sitting in the back of the 4-tonner for up to an hour waiting for others to finish and finish up and then the driving time could take an hour to an hour and a half. That's too long in wet boots or kit when you need to be recuperating for tomorrow's tougher, harder march. Every march, straight away, boots off and foot powder in a big resealable bag that I could just slip my feet into. Shake the bag and the powder covered one foot. Dry pair of tick tocks. Oh, it was like giving your battered and bruised feet a big hug in a sock. Gore-Tex over this so you could put the wet boots on or if you had old trainers in your Bergen put them on, which was probably better because the mountain boots are more than twice their weight when they're basically mobile swimming pools. The instant relief from sorting yourself out in the back of the wagon. Next get a gas stove going, a boil-in-the-bag ration and make a flask of tea. You were on the way to tomorrow's march already feeling better for it. Blokes would just get in, sit there, put some warm kit on or get a sleeping bag out; didn't go the extra bit or change boots or clothing. They never make it. As I said before, when the cold sets in the will sets out.

We were to be marching in Brecon again. The emphasis was on safety. It was total white-out in the mountains. All the goat paths were hidden under 5ft of snow. I was the first to set off from Brecon Reservoir going to the top of Pen y Fan. Jesus, going first was brutal. I was the pathfinder or trailblazer. Thankfully I knew the area well but I couldn't find any paths for love nor money under the white wonderland. Looked romantic all right but try bloody marching with 50lb not including rifle or food or water in that weight. It was a huge extra strain. I had to lift my thigh until it was 90 degrees and kick the bottom half of my leg over the snow. Then down again until terra firma. Then the same with the other leg. As more men marched through it would make a more acceptable compact patch but for the one leading out front, it was surreal the effort you had to put in to get from one checkpoint to another due to the weather conditions. Timings went out the window. We weren't informed about this, just best effort, but we knew our timings were way over the limit. You couldn't accurately gauge at what speed you were traversing the mountains compared to normal conditions. Finish and you made it to the next march. That was epic in itself. Vehicles, men and machines were breaking down in the arctic conditions. I'd never seen it like this before or after.

I reached the top of the Fan. Two lonesome directing staff were inside a tent that was rippling with the wind; it was zipped up to the max to keep the weather out. I gave a shout. They hastily opened the zip. When they heard my voice, or rather accent, ah, they thought, time for some morale; they did look bored. They asked if I was happy. I was covered in snow head to toe. My face had snow frozen to it. I looked like Santa in army fatigues sporting an Irish accent. I replied, 'Fucking delirious, staff.' Just one of those moments that is surreal but funny. I headed on my way. I was going down the other side of the Fan. It's all rock and one slip and you're going to have a rapid descent with an even more rapid full stop. If I slipped I was dead. I looked about, rooting for something to use as a sledge to slide down and save time and energy. I contemplated taking my Bergen off, lying on it and sliding down but it just wasn't aerodynamic enough to use. Pity, because if it had been it was coming straight off my pain-decimated back within milliseconds and the thought of the Bergen carrying me instead, even for a couple of hundred metres down the mountain, was nearly giving me a hard-on. It was just too cold for Twinky Winky to come out and play too.

It was to be a slow trudge through the snowstorm and snowdrifts. I never saw a sinner on those first four marches. The visibility was about 50 metres. Thank God I know the place like the back of my hand, just getting the bearing off the map for the general direction. The weight increased all week. Then it was the last march before the infamous Long Drag or Endurance as others call it. Same march, same effort. We'd run two hours over the cut-off time for finishing. By the time we got back and sorted food, kit and rations for the final endurance march, and with a briefing and the cookhouse as well, we were looking at one hour's sleep if we were lucky. We weren't. Blokes were messing with kit, lads making noise, bodies battered, feet hanging over the beds looking like they belonged to ogres, not fit young men. I was screwed even before I started the march. My back and arms were swelling up. I remember laughing in the cookhouse with some mates about it. It wasn't going to stop me. I ate like a horse. The Bergen weighed in at 69lb not including food, water and rifle (which brought it in at over 80lb). It was snowing, a dark and cold night to be just sitting around on our Bergens at 10.30 pm in the parade square. There was an eerie silence. The only way you knew anyone was there was by the condensation and steam of blokes' breath, billowing out like silent trumpets. For many the 4-tonner seemed to be even more miserable tonight. I tucked into the flask. We were briefed that the waiting time between recruits setting off was cut from five-minute intervals to every two minutes. Didn't want blokes going down with hypothermia before they set off. A few had made the Jack Wagon at the start even before kick-off. They knew what lay in front so to lay behind was the easier option to them. I never judge. To put yourself in the ring to make it that far under those conditions in January/February 2009 was a Herculean feat in itself.

I went forward with the half a house on my back, gave my details and, as before, put one foot in front of the other. The climb was horrendous. Blokes were slipping and going over with nearly half their body weight strapped to their shoulders in a snowstorm. Some never got up, just lay there. Then, when there was a break, they'd pick themselves up and go downhill into history. We all had head torches on. We weren't bothered about the directing staff. Breaking your legs or back was a clear and present danger. The only problem was they highlighted the white bleakness and hardship. As we kept climbing I was surprised by how many were stopping and starting. This was going to be the toughest endurance march in years. It was slow and unrelenting. You would pass two or three blokes grouped together, sitting down, getting their breath back. There wasn't a volunteer who wasn't exhausted by now. Talybont to the Storey Arms. Up and over the Fan. A winter night during a UK-wide big freeze. My back was bent right forward. I couldn't feel from my armpits down to my fingers. I had gloves on but the circulation was buggered. I couldn't eat now. One minute I was sweating, the next shivering. I kept going. Then I vomited. I was in rag order. Another vomiting session. Got some water down me. Kept going. It was killing me to march but I couldn't stop. It was slow but it was moving. I saw some take out their sleeping bags and waterproof liner for the sleeping bag and just get in. I knew it was serious what was going on.

After about five hours' marching I was only making it towards the Fan. I wasn't in front but I wasn't behind either. It took every ounce of strength that was left in me to climb up Jacob's Ladder on the way up to Pen y Fan. Just get it done. You didn't have to summit as there was no checkpoint at the top but the path that's just below was obviously gone in a snow maze. It was hard going circumnavigating the mountain. I was now on the downward slope. Still about 3km to the checkpoint. Still dark, still snowing and still a white-out. Jesus, I was in bad shape but I knew get past Storey Arms and then daylight would soon be arriving. I fell, stumbled and picked myself back up enough times to make a drunk feel sober.

By the time I arrived at the first checkpoint there were at least ten lads wrapped up in sleeping bags. I got to the checkpoint; it was the HQ vehicle. A big van with radios and desks and so forth: mobile command unit. I gave my name etc., where I was on the map and then they gave me the new grid location. I knew where it was; I'd done this march before. They asked for a bearing which is the direction of travel you take with a compass and the map: align the map to the ground around you and take that bearing on the compass. I couldn't move the dial on the compass. My arms and hands had swollen to nearly twice their normal size. They were cold, not yet frostbite but it was coming soon. I was ordered to go to the medic. I protested, saying I was fine and I knew the terrain and route but I was put in the ambulance and checked over. The medic wouldn't let me continue. He and the officer commanding the hills phase said I was in no shape to continue. It was too many checkpoints up in the mountains again before the next road checkpoint and they said my circulation was gone. I begged and begged the officer commanding; I knew he would understand. There were tears running down my face. I said I would be okay. Daylight would be here. He said the weather and snow was the worst it had been for years and it was going to be in for the next few days. He gave me a hug. It was a really decent thing to do. I was screwed; I knew I was screwed but I couldn't quit. I wanted to march or die. The legionnaire spirit was alive and well in Wales. They put me in the ambulance to get the circulation going and warmed up. Then it was back to camp. I was in a state of shock. I had been medically withdrawn.

When I got back to the accommodation there were a few lads laid up in beds. That night had taken a lot of scalps. I packed my kit. I changed into a dry tracksuit. Didn't eat or shower. Fitted the motor up and got in it to go to Hertfordshire. No sleep. I'd just come down off a mountain after four weeks of the hardest physical testing of your limits. I couldn't stay. I should have been out there in the hell of winter, not here in no man's land. I drove out. I went about 20 miles and I couldn't keep my eyes open. I pulled in, left the engine running for heat and passed out at the steering wheel. Dehydrated, back and arms buggered. Thankfully it was an automatic car. I was running on despair alone. I woke a few hours later and continued the drive. By this time, 21, my unit, had heard what had happened. I got a phone call: go straight to Chilwell in the morning. I did. Got home, unpacked and then drove up to Nottingham; Chilwell's not far from the town centre. I went to the administration department. They'd been expecting me. Now I'd thawed out I was in agony. The stinging heat pain in my feet, arms and hands was unbearable, coupled with an injured back. I hadn't taken any painkillers since vomiting on Pen y Fan and boy did I know it. Got my papers and saw the doctor. I was told I needed a few weeks' rehabilitation. I spent the next two months with needles in my back and working on getting my arms and hands back to normal. God, was it demoralizing. I was super fit but the body was screwed from abuse. Jesus, there was still life in it yet though. Once I got signed off to go home after rehab, the first thing I did was return to my barracks in London and put my name down for the summer selection. Damn right, I might have been knocked down but I wasn't knocked out.

I had healed well. I was back into training at my squadron in 21 SAS while training in the mountains on my own time again. I was happy with the progress. Summer selection began in earnest in July. The three-week beast up to test week had changed somewhat, with some of the more infamous beasting days altered. It was just as intense but I did fine. I was known by some of the directing staff; that just goes with the territory. Test week came. Did all my marches including endurance. To pass the Storey Arms at good speed on endurance was tearful. It put an old ghost to bed. I went round the 64km march at a steady pace, no injuries and strong. I even ran over the hot-coal section and tarmac lanes for the last 8 miles like a man possessed, again passing pain-ridden recruits who were crying for relief or hoping that they could levitate, anything not to have to feel the boot hit the ground and the satanic pleasure received to those poor soles of their feet. Oh, this is the only marching season I like. I went across the finish line like a bloody train. Into the back of the 4-tonner; it was like a home away from home. I had been in one consistently since 2006. This was 2009. That included 21 and 22 selection and pre-deployment training. I had a cut-up piece of sleeping mat one-foot square for the wooden bench. That was all the home comfort I needed in the 4-tonner.

We arrived back at Sennybridge Camp elated. It was a cool summer's day, around late afternoon. I sorted my kit and packed some of it into the car. We had a feast fit for a king in the cookhouse after another four weeks of intense mental and physical exhaustion, but I felt strong and delighted. We were confined to barracks as foot and mouth had been prevalent in some areas of the country. We learned there was no weekend leave. Lots of blokes were getting their heads down to sleep. I, on the other hand, decided that after an eighteen-hour march and a full week of test marches a good session of Guinness was in order. Well, it does give you strength, as they say. I went into the NAAFI, the on-camp bar. There were plenty of the directing staff having beers at their own tables. Out of the recruits that had decided to go to the NAAFI, a few had a pint; the vast majority didn't. I walked straight up to the bar, jumped the queue and all. Well I wasn't going in a line behind blokes ordering fizzy drinks and bags of crisps; 2 pints of Guinness please. The first one didn't touch the sides. Remember, I hadn't slept either. Non-stop marching all the way to the bar. That's what got me through the last few miles like a lunatic. I'm going on the piss now. I had the endurance march beaten in my mind. Oh, the NAAFI was what drove me over the line. Jesus, about 12 pints later at closing time even the directing staff had retired; I was in full swing. By the time I got back to the block, lights were out. I had a carry-out of cans; oh, I had no intention of stopping just yet. I had earned it. Put on some good old Irish session music on my headphones in the accommodation and was dancing and drinking while everyone was sleeping. I eventually passed out, exhausted but not thirsty. No hangover the next day. The other blokes said I was hard-core. I replied, 'Why not?' It was nice having down time. I just sorted out my administration and kit ready for the next stay: pre-jungle training near Hereford.

There was no leave or any time off due to the foot-and-mouth crisis. We all drove in convoy to a training facility in Herefordshire. We were billeted in a shed basically. All hands on deck to first clean it out and then set up the folding cot bed for your sleeping arrangements. We all made ourselves as cosy as possible; this was home for the next month. It was basic but compared to what was coming, it was the Hilton. I needed fattening up for the jungle and I didn't hesitate on that. As this training facility was put together as a fast ball due to travel restrictions, it was a tented mess hall and cookhouse. Just like the green army big field exercises. The cooks didn't disappoint again. All you could eat; no rationing here. Fill your boots. Any more for any more?

I was doing light physical training for the first two weeks just to get back into shape and not overdo it. Feet and most other body parts needed regenerating after the Brecon mountains. The days were taken up with briefings and lectures on standard operation procedures, patrolling and all aspects of soldiering. It was a different kind of intense, as you were writing and constantly taking notes to be studied and written up again in a good copy, not the speed-writing of class. Then, during one briefing, we were all handed a questionnaire to fill out. I didn't take much notice. It was a generic one, the type that most recruits fill out in any organization. First few questions were about your name, date of birth, military courses and operations you had been on. Then they got a little more personal. You could see lads taking out their quills and giving Shakespeare a run for his money, writing down what they thought would get them further. The next question was why are you joining the SAS? Most blokes gave a heartfelt bullshit story. I just wrote 'For the craic.' Oh, it gets better. Another few questions, then 'What are your strengths?' I put down, 'Team player, do anything to get it done, selfless, driven, resilient.' The next question: 'What are your weaknesses?' I put down 'jam doughnuts'. Jesus, I didn't foresee what happened next. I handed in the questionnaire. About lunchtime when we all had eaten and were chilling, I heard the roar of my surname. Oh no, I thought, this reminds me of every other time I got up to mischief and the subsequent consequences. One of the directing staff was holding a jam doughnut. 'Since you like these so much, keep it in your top left pocket and have it ready for inspection on a moment's notice. In the exact condition it was handed to you.'

Within a few days we would be flying to Brunei, the other side of the world, to do jungle training. The toughest part of Special Forces training. I got a soapbox and some small resealable bags. All this to place the doughnut in as protection while in the tropical humid heat of the jungle. I made sure it was secured, fastened and airtight. I knew that I, like everyone else in the selection process, was going to go through hell with the physical and mental torture of weeks in the jungle. I would be completely screwed but my jam doughnut was going to be perfect.

Due to foot and mouth, we were all driven to a private part of Heathrow away from the public. They hired a passenger plane to take sixty recruits and directing staff and admin staff. The trolley-dollies, including the gay ones, thought they had died and gone to heaven. A plane full of super-fit Special Forces soldiers. All the directing staff were in first class. Obviously we were in the rear with the gear. No booze either. Bastards. Landed in Brunei. The humidity was heavy. I was sweating within ten minutes of landing. It's an Islamic country and conservative. The Sultan of Brunei has good relations with the UK, with a garrison of Gurkhas also stationed there.

We were coached to our camp. Bed spaces and mosquitoes were waiting for us. This was going to be ruthless. We hadn't even begun to unpack our kit when the roar came be on the parade square wearing your physical training kit in five minutes. We were being treated to daily beasting sessions on the beach to help hasten acclimatization; more like to hasten the weak to fail. I can't describe how draining it was in the humidity and heat. Blokes were dropping like flies. One lad had to be taken straight off the beach when he collapsed with a heat injury; the medics confirmed his body temperature had hit 42 degrees Celsius. He was medevacked back to the UK subsequently and discharged from the army. There were others, but I was too busy making sure I wasn't one of them. These were called beach runs, funnily enough. There was a package of range work and so on before being helicoptered into the jungle to start the long exercise. You had to have your administration so precise. The jungle is a beautiful, enchanting forest but it's survival of the fittest in there; it's claustrophobic, hot, humid, energy-sapping. Constant noise night and day from whatever is out there, and there were some out-of-this-world noises when it got dark and when I say it got dark, you couldn't see anything under the canopy. You couldn't see the sky except for breaks in the treeline, which were rare. You were reduced to existing on the floor like every other floor-dwelling creature in there. Oh, you know the jungle is your master, my friend. This is proper survival soldiering. Stealth movement by day; laid up by night.

The harshness was unrelenting. One of the days is called immediate action day. This is where you're in your patrol of four to six men, depending on how many recruits were left. You have your fighting kit on – that is, webbing with ammunition and grenades, water bottle and so on – and a daysack with either extra water rations or a radio or some other essential kit. All day you are being ambushed and taking casualties in mock scenarios. The heat was deadly. I think we lost nearly twenty blokes that day due to heat or injuries or voluntary withdrawal; that's the three words the directing staff are trying to get you to say: 'I voluntarily withdraw.' They want to break you. I was shoulder-carrying a Gurkha officer. On this drill he was the injured one of our patrol; he was still in but was in bad shape and going downhill rapidly with heat injuries. So we were heaving all the kit in this quagmire as well as these steep ravines. Out of nowhere I heard an explosion. Not a particularly big one. Some directing staff were blowing up trees to make a clearing for the helicopter to come in and winch guys out. Here I am with a lad strung across my shoulders, two rifles and kit going up this near-vertical path up a ravine – known as the Eiger – with directing staff screaming at us and the helicopter 50ft to my left. The co-pilot's eyeballs were popping out at the sight of this Special Forces selection course unfolding below him. Some recruits were lying on stretchers waiting to be hoisted up and being helped by other injured recruits waiting their turn. Some lunatic directing staff was blowing up trees with plastic explosives to clear an opening, all while whoever was still in the fight was putting one foot in front of the other. I have no idea how I got up there, but I bloody well did.

By the time we reached the safe point of the exercise, the officer who I had been carrying had gone down with heat injuries and he was on my goddam back. My five-man patrol was now reduced to two men: me and an Aussie lad. He was on the deck talking like he was from another planet. Some of the directing staff were nervous about the extent of casualties being taken. No matter what, it's the military and shit goes downhill. My directing staff asked if I was okay. The medics were going over the officer. He was unconscious now. I said I was seeing stars but would it be okay to have a quick ciggie during the break? They were astonished I was still standing and let me have one fag in peace. Jesus, I was holding on by a prayer but I held on. That's all you ever need, just faith in yourself to make it. It didn't quell. It got harder and harder as the days passed. Weight loss, fatigue, all the great ingredients to test the mind, body and soul of a man.

By the time we got to the final exercise, we had to break up our bivouac camps and bring the lot to a central position. This was a seven-day exercise of patrolling with all our Bergens and a kit of nearly 100lb a man. It was goddam suicidal lifting. You had to roll into your Bergen, you were that exhausted. We got helicoptered to another area of the jungle to do the exercise. As soon as we'd set off two directing staff told me I wouldn't get to the end of the exercise which ended at the highest point in that part of the jungle. I knew I was buggered but I just kept going. It had to be a 50 or 60km trek through dense jungle up and down – and of course since we're talking SAS here, up to the highest point – all the time patrolling and doing all our SOPs, or standard operating procedures, to the highest standard for jungle warfare. How I made it to the top is beyond me. Others didn't, but I did. I went down with heat exhaustion. My patrol got water into me and I managed to stay conscious. By the time the exercise finished, all to a man collapsed on the deck. Oh, to be at the finish line. Every man had earned his place. Some lads hugged. A directing staff came over and asked about my jam doughnut. It was in mint condition. He gave me a fag to smoke while we waited for the helicopter to arrive. Once on board this small heavy helicopter, with just enough space for men and kit, we were handed the cold tins of beer which the RAF squadron based in Brunei, and that assist in the jungle training, always donated. I was strapped into my seat, doors wide open, gazing down at the jungle canopy that looked like a sea of broccoli, drinking a can of Foster's lager.

Back to the barracks. It took three showers to even look half clean. Oh, food flowed through us like soup owing to the change from rations to normal food. Every man was red with mosquito bite rashes. Trench foot, you name it, we had it. The foot-and-mouth crisis was over and we got a Royal Brunei flight home, too exhausted to flirt with the hostesses. Back in Hereford for debriefing and so forth. Then home. I was delighted to get back home; a big hug from my fiancée helped. Rest and recuperation. Within a few days I got a phone call from a major at 21 SAS asking if I wanted to deploy to Afghanistan in a few weeks. I was out of the jungle and now I was heading back to Afghanistan, getting ready to deploy to Helmand and I couldn't wait to go fighting again, although I took the phone call in the pub. Well, I did go on the piss for a few days after the jungle. Now my mind was on the Stan and explaining to the Mrs that I was going away again. That's life.

Chapter Six

Welcome Back, We Missed You!

The jungle wounds had just about healed when I received my mobilization papers and was instructed to report to Chilwell Barracks. I was well used to the routine. I had been living out of a Bergen now for several years. It was around mid-October. I was still acclimatized to the Brunei jungle weather. I arrived at Chilwell and duly took up my role as a wandering lone soldier going through the various departments again. No big queues this time around. Nice and quiet and quick. All done in a couple of hours. I reported to my barracks in London to sort some kit and weapons to take with me. I would be doing my pre-deployment training in Wales again. I arrived that day and stored the weapons in the armoury. I was attached to the HQ element for pre-deployment training and would subsequently be attached to a rifle company. My role in the task force would be Forward Intelligence Reconnaissance Liaison Officer (FIRLO for short) – sounds even better with an Irish accent – and I would be based out of the intelligence section of the infantry company, or J2 in military-speak. My training would be hard and fast; flexibility is a cornerstone of a Special Forces operator's mindset. I knew how the Afghan mindset worked as well, so I knew no matter how flexible I was I'd need to be a walking rubber band with the patience of a saint to boot. It was refreshing to learn a different role and skillset. Intelligence-gathering is a multifaceted area. It is just amazing what you can glean from basic information alone; we are certainly creatures of habit. I was due to fly out late November/early December. I had a colleague doing the same role, so I would be replacing him and getting all the handovers and his experience in-country which is always better than going in fresh with no handover. Otherwise you lose at least six weeks just getting a feel for the ground. It was the same procedure as before: Brize Norton to Kandahar, night stopover at Kandahar, same palaver with incoming rockets, except this time I didn't budge.

After the last tour this place was like Blackpool in uniform. Plenty of others did budge though. I just couldn't be arsed and besides I had a comfy seat; I wasn't giving that up for a rocket. We jumped on the C-130 and didn't beat the sunrise to Bastion this time either. I had only left eleven months earlier and the place had already mushroomed in size. The US military and their Marines had a camp adjacent: Camp Leatherneck. It was run by the US Marine Corps. Great lads; proper up for a fight too. That film *Jarhead* does them no justice. They're intelligent, loyal and courageous soldiers; very patriotic and conservative. I had briefly worked with Yanks and, unlike the crap television portrays, any I met were down to earth, family- and country-orientated. Conservative people. No brash loudness or any of those media stereotypes. I spent two days waiting to get a lift to the camp where I would be based. It was about a thirty-minute drive from Camp Bastion. It was a lovely little camp surrounded by rocky desert and a nice steep hill for physical training and a good watch position to overlook the surrounding area, and it was away from the prying eyes of any HQ element central like Bastion, or Bullshit Central in Tommy-talk. I settled in quick. Usual stuff: bed space, unpack kit, get a layout of the important areas of the camp; that is, the cookhouse, gym and armoury. That's all a man needs: food, fitness and fighting. The simple things in life are the most rewarding. My role was to mentor, train and escort on the ground an Afghan team. We would be part of a bigger manoeuvre group of about 15 to 20 UK troops and 50 Afghan soldiers; all in, 100 fighting men armed to the teeth and up for a scrap any time.

Although the mission was generally aimed at gaining influence and intelligence, the main task was to access areas in the Central Helmand River Valley where NATO ultimately had little or no presence. I would be at the epicentre of the patrol. My team and I would engage with tribal elders. We'd listen to the village elders and gain information on a whole array of situations and aspects of life in these remote villages, gleaning a sense of who is who, the affiliations, loyalties and needs. We communicated what assistance we could and what we could bring into their sphere of influence: help with schooling or water supplies and so on. We generally received a warm welcome as per the Pashtun tradition, which dates back 5,000 years, long before Islam entered this tribal area. Hospitality is sacred to the Pashtun community. These values have been lost in many Western societies over recent years, more so in the urban areas than in the villages and small towns; it's the big cities that do all the harm. Now I've gone off on a tangent again. Well, while we were chatting, they showed us their hospitality. It's against their code to be anything other than hospitable. They will even protect a visitor or stranger who is in their territory. I cannot stress enough what a truly beautiful place Afghanistan is. A vast array of people and culture and landscape. If any people deserve peace and happiness, it's the Afghans. It would be lovely to return to Helmand and tour all the country in safety as it was before all the outside influence.

We also ran a health clinic from the camp once a month. This camp also had the first veterinary clinic to visit and help local farmers to maintain and treat the sheep and goats. We built a pen for the sheep and had farmers come every month with their sheep to be dosed with antibiotics for better milk yield and weight gain. I used to assist the vet in dosing the sheep. You can take the man out of the country, but not the country out of the man.

My first major patrol would see us leave camp for a few weeks at a time to travel to those areas or where TFH needed something doing fast. We would be going to Nad-e Ali district. I knew that the British element of the NATO Task Force had invested heavily in manpower and capital. It had now expanded considerably from the initial twenty-four-hour patrols it had been involved in during my last tour not even twelve months previously. There was a remarkable difference since the siege. The DC had been transformed and NATO had spread out from the district centre to many areas in Nad-e Ali. My team and I arrived at a forward operating base in Nad-e Ali district. Only a few weeks earlier five UK soldiers had been killed by a rogue Afghan police officer. They were part of the mentoring team to train the police and the Afghan army. I had done that role previously. The Grenadier Guards would be our hosts at the camp. My team and I would be at the forefront of the reconnaissance patrols pushing out into Taliban-controlled territory.

It was now mid-December and all the green foliage of summer had disappeared. Rain and clouds and cold had taken over. We were only in one-man tents; something out of Halfords. It didn't bother me. I was well used to sleeping out under the stars whatever the weather. I had a hammock and a basher, a rain sheet to go over where I was sleeping. My kit and I were dry and warm compared to others; some skills never leave you. I even had an old ammo tin for a stove with a fire. Cosy as a mouse I was. Early in the morning you would get a few lonely wet troops hanging about to warm up. They couldn't believe this Irishman in a hammock in winter in Afghanistan with a little camp fire having the craic with them. As I chatted with a few of the privates from the Grenadier Guards, I could tell the shooting incident was still raw with them; you could tell it hit the place hard. It was decided to do a night infiltration into the area around where the shooting had taken place. We would then carry out a clearing patrol to root out any Taliban and take them on. Once first light came up we would then make our way through the compounds. If there was any sign of life, my team and I would move forward to interact with the locals and to try to organize a *shura*, the Afghan name for an informal gathering, typically of elders or village elders. Before we could even consider that we were contacted. Bullets were whizzing and RPGs flying in both directions.

The Afghan soldiers we had were hungry for a fight. The minute it kicked off they were on it. We fired and moved forward to take on the enemy and move towards clearing the compounds. This went on for much of the morning. Thankfully the Taliban believe in having tea breaks. We'd listen to them over our Motorola radios. I briefed the interpreter in my team to get as much information as he could; I also instructed him to pretend he was the Taliban commander; the Taliban and the interpreter argued and slagged each other off over the radio. Even if it didn't turn out to be effective it was funny, and hopefully it would sow some disarray within the Taliban forces and might slow down their momentum or lead them to give away some locations or information; take them out of their comfort zone. Always take the fight to the bastards.

A lot of these were hit-and-run attacks. During one of the frequent firefights, as we were only a six- to eight-man team, we were light and mobile and were chasing them down. The Afghan members were baying for blood and I had no issue. I loved taking them out too. The intel coming over the radio was these soldiers are like ghosts; they're not the typical soldiers. The Taliban were on the back foot and some of the low-ranking members did not want to come out and play. They were scared. I can assure you we heard this in many areas of the Central Helmand River Valley. If you take the fight to them with such ferocity, it's not what they're expecting. My team was fast, silent and ruthless. If we weren't talking, we were fighting with a vengeance. That was part of the course. The operation went on for a few days. We slept out in the middle of the Taliban's territory, with guard duty and so forth. There was little or no sleep. We met up with a patrol of the Grenadier Guards, all young lads apart from the platoon sergeant; Danny was his name, nice lad, probably 28 or so and he had wisdom beyond his years. His commander, a young lieutenant officer, was just out of Sandhurst. Talk about out of his depth. You could see the panic in his eyes and that of his young charge. In the middle of this hot fight, I was radioing back map coordinates and enemy positions to the HQ element that was set up in the rear to bring our assets and if possible mortar elements to bear on the multiple Taliban positions; there were casualties on both sides. I noticed that some of these lads were going into shock at what they were witnessing. I passed a ciggie to a young lad who had that 1,000-yard stare and the pale complexion of shock. I smiled and said, 'Life's fucking sweet, take a few puffs on that.' Poor lad was dumbfounded. Bullets, rockets whizzing by and I'm all nonchalant about it. It helped him though. You've got to take the seriousness out of it sometimes to be effective again.

Then came the news that the Grenadier Guards had taken some casualties. A pedro call sign; that is, the US army medics on board a Black Hawk helicopter with a .50-cal heavy machine gun. They usually fly in pairs. One lands to pick up the casualties while the other gives covering fire from the air. It's a sweet sight to behold in the middle of battle, watching this bird circle as a coloured-smoke grenade is thrown by the stretcher team on the ground to mark the landing site for the helicopter, the blue smoke pouring out as the Black Hawk lowers to land, blowing the smoke with the rotors into the blue swirling vortex. Sometimes praise for these silent men and women, the medics on board these and other medical evacuations who come in under fire, is not high enough. I take my hat off to these pilots and crew. They're not used to being in the thick of it on the ground in the sort of way we are but that does not deter them one iota. I truly want to thank them for their courage under fire. From a fighting soldier's point of view, to know that when the shit hits the fan and you're in serious shit, as was the case here and on many, many occasions on my tours, there is a comfort in seeing these angels with machine guns descend from the sky to pick up injured men and take them on the road to recovery or sadly to the graveyard from serious injuries.

It was like I was in a scene straight out of *Apocalypse Now*. Eerie. The lieutenant commanding his team was going into battle shock, shouting gibberish orders. Poor young officer's first taste of real war. I got a grip of him, let him know what the plan was and let him give the orders. It's the military; rank is rank. Even when it's against your better judgement, you've got to roll with it. I was only out with my team. The other units can take care of themselves, rightly or wrongly. I then watched in amazement as this young private let off this £62,000's worth of rocket just because he couldn't be arsed to carry it back. I roared with laughter. I patted him on the back. You did right, son. Give it to them big-style, and that was the gusto of operations during the festive period. Christmas morning: I woke in my hammock to a cold, damp Afghan morning. I could see some officers going around the men with tea urns and plastic cups. They were handing out hot port in a gesture of seasonal cheer. The captain of our patrol served me a Christmas drink, a great officer: led from the front and was well up for a fight. Well, it's Airborne all the way.

We returned to our camp a few days later. I spent some time prepping for the next excursion out. For a few weeks we'd be on mobile patrols. We returned to the north-east part of Nad-e Ali. It was the same routine; all the patrols were tasked for gathering intelligence for the big political and military operation, MOSHTARAK. Basically, we were going out talking and gathering information from village elders and so on to gain a picture of who held power in that specific village and where that lay in relation to the district. So, people of influence could be used to steer thinking in a certain manner. Early one morning, while on patrol, my team and I were waiting for first light so we could go knock on some doors. My interpreter heard over the radio that the Taliban were lining up to fire a rocket at one of the vehicles of another patrol. We were on foot, laid up in a ditch. I spotted this figure 200 metres away crouching along a hedgerow with an RPG in his hands. I quickly took a shot and hit him in the shoulder. He crawled towards some wood piles, still holding the RPG. I couldn't get a clear shot so I used the underslung grenade-launcher (UGL) on my rifle and launched a grenade. The first one dropped 50 metres short. I took aim again and bingo. That disintegrated him and the threat.

Now I'd opened up a right hornet's nest. We were being contacted all over the shop. My team and I gave chase to some Taliban. We were at the forefront of the contact. Our patrol numbered seventy men but we weren't the only ones there as we'd joined the local unit in place to hold the ground. There were 100+ men, mortars on standby and an Apache helicopter gunship. The top rank was a major from some British army unit so our commander was outranked. The major decided to halt the fight when we were giving chase, firing and manoeuvring forward. At the time General Stanley McChrystal, the head of NATO forces in Afghanistan, had decreed that 'courageous restraint' when taking the fight to the enemy may or may not do more harm than good. His thinking was that we could lose the general population if there was too much collateral damage going on. What this misguided fool did not take into account was Afghan culture and the fact that Afghans themselves believe in fighting and standing up to the enemy. To the locals, walking away was the worst thing you could do. Many were sitting on the fence, unsure whether to support the Taliban or the Afghan government representatives in Helmand. The tactic of walking away played straight into the Taliban's hands. It would make us wonder if incompetency was being replaced by purposeful screw-ups. Many officers just went along with this without passing the reality of the situation up the chain; that it may look good in a press conference in a heavily-fortified base in central Kabul, but on the knife-edge of Helmand Province it was sheer stupidity. Thank God many of the low-ranking officers in the field were fighting men and carried the fight to the Taliban, come hell or high water. As for the Tommies, well, they never back down, ever. It's us who win the wars; the generals just take the credit a long way back in the rear with political goals in mind.

As my team and I made our way back towards the patrol base at the end of the debacle, I wasn't pleased. I informed the chain of command that the decision was detrimental to any work being done in the area. We certainly didn't take the major out on any other ops or patrols. The tempo of operations was hot, fast and hard. We were at the heart of the reconnaissance through most of the Central Helmand River Valley for Operation MOSHTARAK. We were in the Nad-e Ali district. The area was littered with IEDs. The main issue was that with patrol bases and smaller camps or even compounds, you were static and the Taliban had deployed the tactic of planting IEDs all around and on known patrol routes. It's the same as looking out the window of your house and there's dog shit outside the front door, and more shit on the path or pavement around and near your house. Except this dog shit kills and maims regardless of rank or belief. It wasn't a case of if your patrol would get hit, but when it would strike an IED.

When we set off from the patrol base, we were out at night and would patrol during darkness to reach the objective before first light. This meant we were turning up out of the blue onto the Taliban's doorstep. My team and I were with the platoon sergeant and his team of British and Afghan troops. We came under fire from multiple positions. The platoon sergeant – Pete was his name – and I returned fire from a drainage ditch. The others, who were out of sight, took cover in an unused compound. I vividly remember having a sixth sense about an IED or explosion. As in previous cases, something came into my mind near or a few minutes before some life-or-death situation was about to unfold and there have been more than I care to remember. As Pete and I ran down this hedgerow towards the compound, the troops in the compound were now returning fire to the Taliban. We made it to the entrance of the compound. One of the lance corporals who was leading some Afghans in the firefight told me they had just arrived into the compound. It was a disused compound that had previously been used by the Taliban. As soon as I heard this I instructed one of the two US Marine Corps dog-handlers who were attached to our unit; I briefed him fast on the compound. He let the dog off the lead to search. No sooner was the dog off the lead and bang. I blacked out for a few seconds, coming to lying down. I had been thrown a couple of feet by the blast. My left ear was ringing; my left arm was in pain. I instantly turned to look at my arms and legs; they were all there and working. I looked behind me; there were blokes writhing on the ground, screaming in pain and shock. I roared at everyone not to move an inch. I knew there would be more IEDs in the compound. I radioed to our commander. 'Contact IED. Wait out.'

That was just a heads-up at what was unfolding. The Taliban increased their rate of fire; they knew we were hit and in disarray. Most of the British troops were either injured or dealing with casualties. I ordered a young private to use the mine-detector to clear a path to the injured while getting the two US Marine dog-handlers Tim and Charlie to take the rest of the Afghan soldiers out of the compound and set up a fire base to return fire and cover us from the Taliban while we organized ourselves amid the screaming hell of hurt. The medic and another two lads held Pete down to administer first aid; others attended the other wounded. Beep beep, went the mine-detector. We found a second IED a metre from the casualties. I was on one knee right beside the pressure plate. Safest place. No one was going to step on it with me guarding it. All in all there were several IEDs in that compound.

I organized a stretcher party and gathered the men to move out to a waiting quick-reaction force that was in vehicles coming from the patrol base to take the wounded out of the battle and return them to base to be airlifted to Camp Bastion. All the time we were under fire but the courage and dedication of these very young privates from the Parachute Regiment was truly heart-warming. These young lads just got on with it. Some were in shock but it didn't faze them. One lad called Elliot impressed me. I thought to myself that lad's got SAS written all over him. We made it with the stretcher party to the QRF. They took the injured onwards to Bastion. Pete was airlifted with the other casualties. I'm unsure how he fared. Half our call sign was combat-ineffective. We waited for the other half to regroup and return to base, to reorganize and make sure kit and personnel were okay. I didn't know at the time but our patrol commander put me forward and wrote me up for my actions that day. In my eyes it was all a team effort. I just happened to react first and shout the orders. I couldn't have done anything on my own. It was the lads and I who did it together, not me on my own.

Once the dust of battle had settled and we waited for replacement troops to be sent in, it gave us all time to gather our thoughts. It's a shit time when a patrol gets hit badly. You pull each other through and keep focused on the objective. A few sobering thoughts and then get on with it. I spoke with the captain. 'This place is littered with IEDs,' I said. The whole radius around the area had been planted. We would need to push through the ring of IEDs into new ground for any freedom of movement; otherwise we were in a killing zone. Basically, the Taliban would observe us and then make contact with small arms or RPGs. Knowing your tactics and how the troops would react, they would just lure you in, hit you so you would be channelled into an IED pit and then the IED strike would come, and then the next onslaught from the Taliban when you're at your weakest. Great and simple tactic. Very effective and very messy.

Many a soldier's blood drained away into the thirsty Helmand clay; dry red pain drops attracting flies to feast. The next patrol was out at dark o'clock again. We pushed further into the Badlands. By the time we reached our objective it would be first light in an hour. Most of the patrol was stretched along this wall; it was pitch black. We were all using night-vision goggles. Some of the Afghan soldiers found a command wire, an electric wire that goes from a battery to an IED. Most IEDs are like a land-mine - that is, when you step on them, they detonate - but with a command wire the enemy detonates the IED instead of the victim. We found the IED and it was huge. It was twilight time – not dark, not light – but you could make out buildings and shapes; we were outside a compound with a perimeter wall. Next thing we found another IED. It was now apparent that we were in the middle of an IED ambush. This was the killing zone. The open ground outside the compound and wall was where you would be hit by gunfire if the Taliban was awake. Or it was there that later in the day troops would run for cover behind the wall, right into ambush. The enemy would detonate the command wire at one end of the wall and then, as men would make their way down the wall in the opposite direction to escape with the injured, a second IED would inflict mass casualties. I found two IEDs 2ft away from me and with another lad made a safe passage for everyone. The whole patrol passed between us as we stood beside the IED pressure plates. There is a lot to be said for night infiltration. Jesus, that place was spooky. It was designed for death. We marked the compound. Later joint direct attack munition (JDAM) or some 2,000lb bombs would make it safe. Later that day we did meet the Taliban, and a sniper and I were taking shots off a rooftop while our opposite numbers were returning the favour. Oh, the sweet taste of gunpowder and vengeance rang through the air. We had to call in artillery support when it heated up big-time.

The artillery comprised big 120mm pieces and these were stationed at the patrol base 4km away. It was a very short distance for the artillery to be used but we had no mortar team with us. As we fired and manoeuvred back, the village comprised clusters of houses and rat-runs; you couldn't get to the enemy without taking significant casualties. The artillery shells were hilarious to hear. It was like cannonballs thundering past you towards the target. The artillery guns must have been nearly horizontal because they were flying past us only a couple of feet above our heads. Jesus, the destination must have been a shithole after these landed. It was like the Battle of Waterloo with them barrelling down the field towards the enemy. That's just the way the cookie crumbles. Thankfully we made it out of that part of the world on a Chinook back to camp.

After a few days of preparing vehicles, kit and supplies and training the Afghan soldiers for the next excursion, it would be another few weeks behind enemy lines or, as sometimes the case may be, TFH Command Centre if the crack-smoking staff officers managed to wrangle us away from our taskings to assist them. Oh, they like using units like play toys. Don't even ask me what the hell we or for that matter the ordinary infantry soldiers were doing. Some bigwig was going to clear out the Taliban and open up 500 metres of dirt track so it would look good on paper and funnily enough a camera crew was on tour. My team and I were attached to an infantry unit with the rest of our patrol; we pushed through the night to take positions up past the front line. We were going to have a *shura* with the local village elders once daylight arrived, to reassure them and ourselves that apparently we knew what we were doing. Most of the time fact was stranger than fiction. We arrived before first light to the local elder's compound. He had been asleep but not any more, once we had invited ourselves in and secured the place.

We were guided into the guest room of the compound for some chai (tea) and warm bread. We were not to be seen by anyone. We were just lying low for the main event and then would work it from there. We were delighted. We posted some sentries and the elder and I chatted via an interpreter. It was cold and wet outside, but mid-winter in Helmand is not like that in the highlands of the north Afghanistan that are part of the same range as the Himalayan mountain range that sweeps west to the east through Iran, Afghanistan, Pakistan, India, China: beautiful and remote. It was comfy sitting down, sipping chai while we defrosted. The main event was an engineer unit would use a mine-clearing machine to clear the track from the military outpost to the crossroads that the compound was beside. The mine-clearing machine is a vehicle with instruments to detonate the IEDs or mines at a safe distance in front of the protected driver. Then, boom: the explosion rang out and the place reverberated. The mine had hit an IED designed for a vehicle; most likely a couple of 150mm shells from an old Russian artillery from their schmooze cruise in the Stan. I heard in my earpiece that the driver of the mine-clearing machine had broken his shoulder from the shockwave of the blast hitting the vehicle. If he had been directly on top of it, we'd have been mopping him up with a sponge. Though the machine is designed for the job, you still get injured. Defeats the purpose. The machine was injured too.

Back to basics: a foot patrol was deployed; men with the world's most overpriced metal-detectors. It was light and even the man in the moon knew NATO was out patrolling this morning. I went out for a look to see the show. I peered through a door and up the road were vehicles full of men advancing at a steady pace. Now the interpreter was hearing on the walkie-talkie that the Taliban were up and getting ready. Ah, there'll be no talking again today, I thought.

I could see the foot patrol with the blokes using the hand-held mine detectors. They were clearing the road inch by inch. They found and marked another IED. Everything would come to a halt while they waited for the engineers to come and check it out and either make it safe or blow it up in situ, whichever was best. Only problem was, I had now been made aware that accompanying the high-ranking officers was a camera crew in a vehicle that was shielded from most threats. It weighed nearly 30 tons. We went back to chatting to the compound owner while the engineers went to work. After about two hours the countdown for a controlled explosion went through the radio headset. I informed my team and the occupants of the compound that it was going to get noisy. There were young children there. I told their older siblings to cover the young ones' ears. Three, two, one, boom. It was even bigger than the last one. The anti-vehicle IEDs or mines were enormous. You could only imagine the damage and destruction to any vehicles and people in them. The poor children were scared. The old man told us he had lost a son to one of those bombs and he had been on to the authorities for ages to take them away. He had been threatened by the Taliban but, on the same note, this bloke was a known Taliban sympathizer, if not commander; that's why we weren't being hit yet. We were sitting with their commander. Smiling and joking; that's just the way it went. I would have the craic with them, then we would fight. Bit like being in the pub, but with no beer.

As the day drew on I went outside the compound to watch the explosive search team walking along the road, slowly checking for signs or detection of IEDs. I stepped inside the compound wall and within minutes there was another explosion about 5 metres from me on the other side of the wall. I instantly knew this was not planned; there is the unmistakable smell after an explosion and that sinking feeling. There was smoke and dust and commotion everywhere. The young lad who was clearing the path had just stepped outside the clear lane and detonated an IED. It blew him into a canal about 10 metres over the other side of the road. His comrades were in shock and had been blown off their feet. We couldn't get out. The Taliban opened up at the same time. As men returned fire, some of the engineers who were in the explosion jumped into the canal to pull the lad out. He had lost legs and arms and was bleeding heavily. In their shock they pulled the casualty to the far bank as we roared as loudly as possible over the gunfire to drag him to the near bank and get tourniquets on his stumps to arrest the massive haemorrhaging. This bloke was minutes from dying. They pulled him up on the far bank; it is what it is. These poor souls had just been in an explosion. Disorientated, they did their best. Now the shouting to put tourniquets on quick was deafening. I couldn't hear the gunfire. Men were willing them to pull him back from death. I'd never felt so helpless. I was only metres away but it might as well have been another country. Some of the soldiers we were attached to got a ladder to make a bridge across the canal to go to his aid. The fortified vehicle with the officers and the TV crew were right next to it now. The cameraman was trying to get a shot out of the window. All of us were sickened at the sight. Here were these tourists wrapped up in their protective bubble observing a firefight and the aftermath of an IED strike from a cocoon. Another reality of war. Carnage on the outside; oblivious ignorance on the inside. Sadly the boy died shortly afterwards of his injuries. He didn't make it back to a platoon house compound 500 metres up that newly-liberated dirt track. He was put in a body bag and on a helicopter for repatriation out of Afghanistan. Home to another broken family. That's war for you. It may be desensitized by computer games, movies, politicians and the money-chasers, but it's not desensitized for those involved at the sharp end. As they say, truth is the first casualty of war. That was part of the course for me on numerous days. I've been too close to death, either delivering it to the enemy or they delivering it to us.

I was exhausted by this stage. My R&R was coming up. I would be flying out of Bastion to Kandahar and then on to Brize Norton. Operation MOSHTARAK was all over the worldwide news before it was launched. I don't recall any other big operation like OVERLORD or the like being broadcast. So the enemy knew everything in advance. I was going to be in the pub in Ireland while the Taliban were on R&R too. I knew there would be no big fight or push. Some 15,000 troops from NATO and the Afghan army and we were 100 men doing the reconnaissance in all the areas they would be going into. Just 100 compared to 15,000 and in front of a camera crew and the whole nine yards; 100 vs 15,000. By Christ, we were lucky bastards. The Taliban were there when we were. Oh, it was amazing craic. They were popping up everywhere and we were engaging them left, right and centre. That's the best thing about being surrounded; you shoot in every goddam direction. The big operation was pure shit on telly. I was toasting the Taliban as I was flat out of Guinness and whiskey. I winked at the telly. 'Don't worry,' I muttered to myself, 'I'm coming back and back with a vengeance.'

R&R is over before it begins. No time for goodbyes. I've had a lifetime of those already. I was back in the Stan now. Emotions were left at the front door of the house in Hertfordshire. I was a cool, calm, calculated, ruthless fighter now. Kill or be killed. I was tasked with going with the Danish military now for a bit. I liked it. They were chilled out, a bit like heavy-metal rockers in uniform: beards, long hair, dreaming of the old glory of the Vikings or they were simply heavily reliant on their reserve element so were a bit more relaxed on the shaving regulations. Now the female soldiers… Jesus, some of them would break you in half. The others – blonde, Nordic and fit – oh, just what a man needed to see for morale from time to time. I never spoke or flirted. I was leading highly-trained Afghan soldiers; it's not part of their culture and I had to respect that and the female soldiers too. Only eye candy back at base after a mission out on the ground. There is no gender: you're either a good soldier or a bad soldier. I've never met a bad female soldier. Hats off to you girls. Many have more balls than some of the men I've seen on my travels fighting up and down Helmand over the years. The Danes' main base was Camp Price just outside Geresh. It was on the main highway linking Camp Bastion and Lashkar Gah, the provincial capital. Like Camp Bastion, it was not in a built-up area but mainly surrounded by desert. I liked Camp Price, especially as it was run by the Danes. Its nickname was Camp Nice. Oh, it was chilled and had lots of eye candy. As per usual my team and I were tucked away in a quiet section as we usually didn't use the cookhouses; we ate with the Afghans, cooked their food and so on.

There was a lot of mistrust between the Western military units and their Afghan counterparts, although these well-trained Afghan soldiers were at a different level and had a selection process to obtain membership. It was irrelevant to a lot of rank and file in camps that never went outside the wire; a few times my team were refused entry to cookhouses. I ended up in arguments, especially as I generally re-educated higher-ranking NCOs over the fact that they were guests in Afghanistan and their camp was pitched on Afghan soil. I understood the mistrust with the green on blue, as it's called: the military term for attacks by indigenous (green) forces on NATO (blue). There were rogue elements in the Afghan police and regular army but we were dressed and acted differently; they knew we were just trying to get a hot meal before we made our way to the next battle. Jealousy is a bittersweet emotion.

Now we would be launching our patrols into the upper Geresh Valley, the unoccupied territory between Geresh and Sangin in the Green Zone. This was where most of the Taliban hid out, especially the foreign fighters in Helmand. We would be welcoming them back to Helmand for the annual spring offensive. As soon as the mountains between Afghanistan and Pakistan were passable after the winter snows, they would migrate back. Incidentally it would coincide with the poppy season, to open up trade and drug routes. Well, you can hardly think ideology is fuelled for free, no matter whose ideology is now being peddled.

As the Danish military were the battlespace owners for this part of Central Helmand River Valley we would sometimes carry out joint operations, or be on our own but with input at the planning stages from the Danes as they would be doing the ground-holding after we left anyway. We arrived by Chinook early morning at a Danish patrol base. Great helicopters, absolute work horses. We were packed in like sardines. Once there, we set about sorting some sleeping spaces and so forth. We would be operating out of this place for a while. It overlooked the Green Zone from the edge of the desert. Very 'close' country, the Green Zone; it was March/April so everything was starting to bloom or boom. It was like the jungle in places with visibility down to a few feet and even less in dense undergrowth. It was cold but humid. Sometimes you thought you were in the Middle Ages or Middle Earth, with the mud huts and clay-reinforced walls about 2ft thick. Bloody strong. Took a fair bit of explosives to breach a hole in a wall, never mind dropping munitions from fighter jets on a compound to hit the enemy. Some of these old forts and compounds were hundreds of years old. They'd stood the test of time better than the history books. The Danes were chilled to work alongside; different mentality fighting-wise though. I don't think the political stage back home had much support so they tried not to get involved. That was for the politicians and the very senior military safe in Copenhagen sipping Carlsberg. The men and women on the front weren't shy about taking it to the Taliban but when casualties mounted, as they do in any war, the tools in suits get wobbly knees first, thousands of miles away, bless them.

We pushed out, passed the usual patrol routes and area of influence, and into territory that certainly wasn't government of Afghanistan- or NATO-friendly. A lot of poppy fields here. So the enemy was more concerned about their income than anything else. My team and I certainly were in a lot of contacts and prolonged firefights here. Jesus, there was fuck all talking here. Ah well, sometimes a picture paints a thousand words. With the amount of ammunition sent in both directions you could have opened an art gallery or library. On one patrol we pushed deep into Taliban country at night and popped up at first light as usual. On the Taliban radio that the interpreter was listening in on he could hear the chorus of disapproval. You know you're in deep when they're tearing new arseholes out of each other to get into position before 6.00 am. Sweet, some hard-core fighters who had alarm clocks. I was on top of the world. Don't get me wrong, a bad day in the office in war is very shit, but when you're on the attack and taking them down like it's going out of fashion, it's exhilarating. Maybe it's that primitive part of the brain. Survival of the species, but by God, do you get a hard-on at the thought of more fighting and it was there for you, as much as you could handle and more.

I had positioned myself and some of the Afghan soldiers along a small ditch and among some trees. I could smell the fight in my nostrils. We spotted shitloads of the bastards, crawling into positions. I radioed back to the forward air-controller, essentially the person responsible to talking to the air on station and coordinating with troops on the ground to get the air to drop on positions located through maps and visually confirmed on the ground. High pressure at high speed. Our man was from the RAF, mid-40s and bald but cool under pressure. Nice fella actually. Always had a brew after a patrol with him. I passed on the coordinates to get the aircraft with the optical instruments to have a closer look. The mortar fire commander was also informed. They were back from our position with the command element of the patrol. All assets were coming to bear on this scrap. I even gave the team a pep talk as we had time; we were ambushing them for a change. Oh yeah, baby. That is how I got them bloody stirred right up for this one. I said 'Right, listen in…' – this was to the British troops, the US troops and the Afghan forces and interpreter; the Danes were sitting these fights out – '… fuck General McChrystal and fuck courageous restraint. The minute these cunts pop up, give it to them with fucking everything you have. Send them into the next world with fucking enthusiasm.' Then I roared 'Mike, foxtrot, victor' (that's the phonetic alphabet). 'MFV.' Even louder now. They were baying for blood. The Afghans were nearly coming in their pants at the thought of being let off their leash. 'Mike, foxtrot, victor. Maximum fucking violence,' I roared, and with that the Taliban introduced themselves bang on. There was some amount of ordnance going in all directions. I was confirming targets to the air-controller and mortar-controller. Within minutes, boom, boom, the mortars were coming in on target from the base a few clicks back from our position. It was as romantic as you could get for a fighting man. I was in love. I don't know how many scratches on the bedpost I got that morning but I was smiling through. The Afghan lads were unstoppable; they were literally salivating around the mouth while launching RPGs at the Taliban positions. It was one of the most intense firefights I'd had the privilege of being in. The fighter jets were on target and the mortars were dropping. Everything was in symphony. A good old-fashioned tear 'em up.

Once it was all done and dusted, positions cleared, we made our way back through the Green Zone jungle, up the inclines into the desert high ground and back to base. When we walked back in the Danes were in shock; the whole upper Geresh Valley had heard that fight. They thought we were mad and they were right. Mad for it. Many patrols and operations up along this part at Upper Geresh went in the same fashion. This was one of my last big scraps before being re-tasked to go with the Yanks. This area was only a kilometre from the last one I described. Same craic again: we moved in under darkness. This place was like being back in the fifteenth century only it had dodgy mobile phones and the people were big into smoking joints and opium. The poppy fields have a purple haze as the morning dew evaporates with the heat of the rising sun in the east and the warm air expands and pushes the cold air west before the sun gets up over the horizon. We were surrounded by poppies. All this opium growing, waiting for us back home where it would eventually end up, in Western Europe as a symbol of war of the soul. Another symptom of war: a war within.

We knocked on a few doors before the early-morning call to prayer. Eventually, we got chatting with the elders. It seemed a bit surreal but were given some chai, made some small talk and tried to organize a *shura* for later that morning. One or two seemed eager but Afghans can be difficult to read, even for our Afghan forces who were usually from the north of Afghanistan. You didn't get many Pashtuns but we had a few and not even they could read them every time. So we went for a patrol around the small hamlet of compounds just to see what was about. The Taliban radio was in full swing so it was just a matter of time before formalities and we were back in the game with them. You may think I don't like the Taliban, but I don't like or dislike them; I respect anyone that stands and fights, irrespective of the cost; a man who fights to fight. The hamlets were in thick undergrowth under trees, with small streams and drainage ditches. We were about 2km inside the Green Zone from the desert edge, which was up on the high ground. Visibility was about 15ft at best. A section of the patrol just got contacted by small-arms fire. Just a test really. They saw it off easily. We made our way through the vegetation to the next house. There were some old men, maybe in their late 50s. They look a lot older; Afghanistan even ages the tourists fast. Some of the Afghan forces called to them to stop to chat. They ignored us and just walked in between the hamlets as we moved on. Next thing, bullets were flying at the front of the patrol that was making its way out of the Green Zone. We were about a kilometre behind them. We were the last element on our way out. The cheeky bastards had got between us and were firing at the front of the patrol that had snaked around the hamlets. As the Taliban – or more precisely the ten-dollar Taliban; they're paid to fight just for work; not much skill but anyone can be lucky – attacked, the front element returned fire to the enemy position. The only problem was that from where we were, we couldn't engage as the bullets and RPGs could potentially hit our own troops. We took cover behind a wall in the hamlet; that's when we figured out where the ten-dollar Taliban were: only a couple of metres in front behind another wall, firing through holes in the wall, which were aptly called 'murder holes'. We went silent. I couldn't risk radioing our command to let them know our position so they could move their fire away from the enemy to allow us to go into the compound to give them the good news and surprise them. I got a foot up to peep over the wall to see where they were so we could throw a grenade in there, break down the door and go in all guns blazing. By this time our front element had set up a fire-support team on the high ground overlooking the Green Zone; they couldn't see us due to the vegetation.

I can assure you that when you get RPGs, small-arms fire and machine-gun fire from your own troops you realize just how well-trained we are. Fuck me, was it accurate. Jesus, I couldn't make myself any smaller. The grenade got popped and so did the ten-dollar Taliban. We got on the radio to give our position. Thankfully the friendly fire – which is not one bit friendly – moved on to other targets. We pushed through. Now the middle element of the patrol was trying to get out of the Green Zone. As usual we had stirred up a hornet's nest. We would take the fight to them as much as possible and then withdraw. We were usually a reconnaissance element so there wasn't much support or ground-holding capability. On the other side of a wall, towards the exit of the Green Zone, some Taliban had laid an IED in a cooking pot with a command wire attached. It was positioned where the patrol would have to jump over to make their way up to an exit point and on to the high ground through a small ravine going up the vertical cliff to the desert. A young lance corporal from Scotland, blond-haired lad for a change, jumped up on the wall; somehow he saw the IED had been placed at the other side of the wall and fell back behind the wall. The Taliban detonated the cooking pot. No one was injured; the wall took the blast. They thought the patrol was passing it. The Scottish lad was in shock, though it didn't deter his skill in using profanities in his thick Scottish lilt; cunts this and cunts that.

We now knew that our escape route had more IEDs. Thankfully the mortar team from the base was sending their love all the way to them. The mortars were now landing in the middle of us as we had been pushed off course by the IED and the subsequent fighting. I said to the new platoon sergeant – Damo was his name – that I'd get a grip of the Afghan soldiers if he would correct the mortar fire. He was a tall lad with glasses and black hair; from the north of England somewhere. I roared at our and the Afghan troops to start pushing for this near-vertical cliff. It was the only viable option; I went with my instincts, as all the obvious routes out were most likely laid with IEDs. I thought better to try to climb out of it than be blown out of it. We had a strong fire-support team on the high ground; the bullets were whizzing very close from both sides. I led from the front. To get some speed into the move I fought up nearly to the top, got a firm hold and then ordered and commanded men to move up to my position and then on to the high ground. It was exposed as hell, but options weren't options at this time. A sniper would have crushed us. The bullets were pinging round my feet. Jesus, did I abuse the shit out of every soldier getting up that cliff with motivation by cursing. Blokes were ducking and diving to make the climb. I went down twice to carry two wounded Afghans up the hill. I got them up thankfully, only twisted ankles and the like. How we weren't carved up I don't know. Speed and aggression are a winning combination.

Once we were all on high ground behind cover I spoke with our commander to inform him we were all safe and that unless we were going back into the Green

Zone it would be best to get off this exposed height before they zeroed in on us with everything they had. We moved back further into the desert. My team and I were at the rear of the long snake of men. The air-controller was co-located with me as was Damo, the platoon sergeant. The air-controller was talking over his radio to the jet on station. They could see the Taliban in the ravine I had chosen to avoid; they were digging around another IED or seeing if it was working. I decided to take the steep cliff option. I knew it was exposed but it wouldn't have any IEDs. Bullets are bearable; bombs are messy. The pilot informed us he couldn't drop any bombs on the enemy owing to courageous restraint again. I snapped at the air-controller, 'What? The air won't strike?' 'Okay,' I turned to Damo, 'Let's get the cunts.' With that he radioed our captain and gave him my quick battle orders to check these were okay. Fair play to the captain, he gave the green light. We dropped every bit of kit, carrying only rifles, bullets and grenades. We were going to be sprinting nearly 800 metres to ambush these Taliban fighters, who were setting up another IED. The pilot had also identified weapons. Tim, the US Marine dog-handler, and Charlie, the other dog-handler, led the way, checking for explosives as we ran as fast as we could to get to them. Within minutes we were there, all of us carrying about 60lb of kit, which wasn't including what we'd left with the air-controller and some others back in the desert. We surprised the life out of the enemy, literally. As they raised their AK-47s to return fire, they got the good news and dropped away. Our Afghan sergeant major ran down, in the middle of the firefight, to grab one Taliban who had put his hands up. He was the only one who made it. The rest decided to raise their weapons and fire. Big mistake. I'm too ruthless to forgive or forget.

We took the prisoner back for formal interrogation. He was in the Afghan forces' hands; he was singing like a canary. By the time the Royal Military Police picked him up from the camp, he had disclosed a whole array of IED bomb-makers and facilitators, locations and the lot; that call to go back paid dividends in saving lives in the future. Some high-ranking generals heard about my exploit, that the air would not drop on the enemy, that my team and I had dropped everything and ran to do the job ourselves. In their praise they said we needed more of this kind of action. I'd been doing this since 2008; it was now halfway through 2010. The crack-smoking officers at the top table in Kabul or any other capital city in the West haven't a clue how to win a war, or more to the point, they don't want a victory; there's no money in peacetime. They seemed to be more of a hindrance than the Taliban.

After that operation, we returned to our camp. There were only a few weeks left in the tour now. Most of the company was prepping the RIP, Relief in Place, with the Marine unit that would take over the role. I, on the other hand, was in full flow. I had volunteered to take another team of Afghan forces out on the ground. I was tasked with compiling a report on the efficiency and results of the Afghan forces and their mentor being allocated alongside other military units. They would be attached to these units, taking their orders from the host unit. A small team like the 'Tiger Teams' we trained and advised out on the ground; they were subject to some tough times with other unit commanders and the end result was generally a waste of the asset that had been donated to them; they were simply used to knock on doors instead of letting their teams do hit-and-run attacks on the Taliban to hinder the enemy's freedom of movement. Many commanders lack the initiative to think outside the box when it comes to war-fighting or counter-insurgency.

We travelled like bums hitching lifts off helicopters and generally sweet-talking our way about. It was nice to have carte blanche; just radio in a situation report nightly or, if we were attached to a green army unit, I would just jump on their radio and give base a quick heads-up. We were left to our own devices. I tried in vain several times to persuade command that small teams like mine should wear Afghan clothing to be able to mingle and take the freedom of movement away from the Taliban where we were operating. The last two weeks of the tour we were in Now Zad in northern Helmand. I had been operating in most of Helmand on and off for three years. We were attached to a US Marine unit on the outskirts of Now Zad. The small town had been completely abandoned when the fighting broke out. We caught a flight on a Marine bird, the one that takes off like a plane and then the rotors rotate upwards to fly as a helicopter. Noisy and slow, mainly.

We arrived at a desolate landing strip with sod all there that you could moan about. As usual, no one knew we had been tasked or that we arrived. I don't have to tell you. Americans really struggle with any accent that is not American and my lilt seems to perplex them even more so, but they did smile a lot. Either they were delirious or intrigued. The route into Now Zad was covered with a fine dust like the dry powdery sand at the top of a beach; it's great when it's dry but it gets everywhere. There had been a lot of IEDs planted and struck by vehicles patrolling this area. They were so prolific that the Marines decided to position vehicles every 1 kilometre or so, all within eyesight of the next vehicle and manned twenty-four hours a day to guard the route. I had been assured it was safe; it didn't bother me anyway. I think they were saying that because they had put ten vehicles in static positions with four men in each and then resupplied them. The commitment alone had to ensure it was safe.

We were about a kilometre from reaching our new task in the district centre. Sodding boom again. I couldn't see a thing. The explosion's shockwave had dispersed the moon dust that was the soil on the dirt road everywhere; it was like a miniature sandstorm. I could feel my toes and was conscious. No screaming either. Jesus, I thought, that was close. The vehicles had been designed so that a blast would blow parts of the vehicle away but the cab with the occupants would be secure. I was a little shocked but okay. Some of the Afghan soldiers had sustained minor injuries to their backs and legs but no serious trauma; it was more from the jolt and impact inside the cab and from the loose kit flying about. We got out; one of the supposed vehicles doing static duty was 400 metres away. They must have been sleeping on the job. It is what it is. It came over the radio that they thought it was a command wire-detonated IED. The Marines in the other vehicles took off like lunatics. I checked over my team and assessed their injuries.

We were one week away from the end of tour. Most blokes were back in the bases, packing and getting the new relief in to give them a handover. I was still out getting blown up again and fighting. I took the initiative and led my team into the base. The Marines found nothing in their chase. I knew they wouldn't. Once we settled down I visited the command part of the Marine unit we were there to patrol with; they hadn't been informed. The officer in charge was a little vague; it sounded like we were going to be used as bait or cannon-fodder. They didn't use half the tactics we used or any of the counter-IED drills, which was fairly bloody obvious from the welcoming committee that had decided to blow us up upon arrival. Cheeky bastards, the Taliban. You've got to hand it to them: right under their noses they planted it. Hats off for balls. I spoke with Afghan soldiers; they were in no mood either. They were due to have leave in a few days; they were living and fighting as a day job. We would arrive every six months, motivated to the clouds with ideas to boot; no wonder they were burned out. I was by this stage. I said I'd make up some shit and sack it off. With three days before I was due out I hadn't the heart to take them out on some foray that was ill-planned and with bad soldiering skills; it was a recipe for a calamity. You know when not to push your luck when you've been about.

We returned to our camp on the day I was supposed to be flying home. That moved to the right. I had to fill in this report and so forth: handover, the lot, no down time. I did what I was supposed to do, including saying my goodbyes to all I had served alongside. The incoming major, who was the officer commanding the task, nearly fainted when I told him I was due out. A part of me was about to volunteer for another crack of the whip but once you have the picture of getting on that freedom flight and getting back to Blighty, it's hard to change your mind. I spoke with the outgoing officer commanding our task force. He informed me that we had been involved in the most hours of contact in combat and it topped the table for TFH. That's twice I had been involved in the most fighting in Helmand. I was sad to be leaving and unsure what the future held after Cameron and his boyfriend were making out in the rose garden in London, telling us that operations would finish by 2014. That just screwed the whole thing. The Taliban must have thought these muppets in the UK can't do anything right. Lions led by donkeys, as the saying goes.

I was in one piece, but I had a small injury from the IED incident back in February that wouldn't heal. I was thirsty and missed my fiancée too. It was now June 2010, summertime in the UK. I landed at Brize, headed straight to the barracks in London, handed in my weapons to the armoury and met with some of the lads. It was then home to Hertfordshire and a big hug from the missus. Went back to barracks in the morning. Usually you get a few days' down time before you're called back. Since austerity was the new buzzword the MOD pen-pushers were salivating there would be no days' grace to rest at home before next orders. I was asked to do a course with two days' notice. I wasn't prepared for it; I'd been back just twenty-four hours. Since I had no course to attend or operation to go on, I would be demobilized. I did go to Chilwell and therein lies the issue: more bullshit from pen-pushers nowhere near a war zone. Civilians in uniform.

Chapter Seven

Cutbacks Cut

I was apprehensive. I certainly wasn't in a UK mindset owing to the fact I was only just out of a war zone. I really could have done with a week or so at home to unwind and chill. I was still highly-coiled from battle. I was unsure also of how to deal with the injury on my elbow; it wasn't a massive issue but it did need sorting. I knew if I just left it I'd have problems with it later down the line. I wouldn't have much room to manoeuvre with any claims for support; they're always looking for a get-out clause. A good friend who is a patrol medic advised me to get it seen to and get it on record just for assurance. I felt guilty though. I'd seen men with far, far worse injuries. Also I hadn't been maimed like them, even after being in three explosions at less than 10ft from the device, 2ft being the closest and nothing.

It's only now I realize that my injuries were non-visible injuries. I don't call it mental health; I'm trying to steer us away from that. The term has been polluted over time. A fresh start is required and the wording non-visible injuries sums it up best. Injury means temporary. I wish I'd known this at the time of arriving in Chilwell. I whizzed round the different sections. I left the medical and administration until the end. I did my hearing test and same problem again: ears were still ringing and are today from explosions and gunfire, even with them being partially covered at the time. I passed somehow, most likely by again pressing the trigger like I was possessed. As I waited to see the doctor it felt different; there was a hint of animosity towards the returning soldiers. The more seriously wounded would have been airlifted out of Afghanistan and straight to Selly Oak, but some of those with minor injuries, especially ones needing physio and so on for several weeks before they were back on their feet, were having to fight tooth and nail to receive any form of treatment. Obviously MOD Whitehall don't want to cut back on defence deals even if they're being ripped off, but will fuck the Tommies straight away to save pennies, not pounds. All these 'remps', rear echelon mother-fuckers as the US Marines on the front line would call them or, to us, those 'in the rear with the gear', while we're running low on ammunition, food and lives, they're fattened pigs, protecting their interests.

I was called forward to see the doctor, a chubby middle-aged balding man from Greece. I knew he was just a hired-in locum. All the military likes outsourcing too. He didn't seem that competent to me. The elbow was deformed and inflamed; he said it would subside. I disagreed, and after a battle of wills I was given the chance to seek a second opinion. The following week I had an appointment at the Park Hospital outside Nottingham, very near to the police HQ. The specialist was a Scottish professor. He took a quick look and had it X-rayed. He advised I needed surgery to sort out the bone disfigurement and clean up the pouch that was accumulating under the elbow. I was relieved; at least it would be sorted. I was on light duties at my barracks in London until the date of the surgery.

Meanwhile my fiancée was organizing our wedding; I had time to help and it offered a welcome distraction to the whole waiting game. I don't know where people get the idea that organizing a wedding is stressful. I thought it was a breeze, from sorting venues to flowers, table covers, music and so forth. Don't get me wrong, once all had been whittled down to two or three options, my fiancée would ultimately make the so-called joint decision. Anything for peace, eh? I received the date of the surgery in the post: August 2010. The date was fast approaching and I was relieved. I figured I would be on the mend in time for the wedding in October of that year. I can tell you being on light duties in barracks is a pain in the arse, especially when you are so used to being in the thick of it. Busy and fit, now bored and restless.

I vividly remember driving up from Hertfordshire to have surgery on a Saturday morning. I arrived in good time, fasting all night and morning. Orders are orders. The procedure was carried out in a private hospital to cut the waiting time. As I waited for the consultant to come and speak to me, one of the staff delivered the bombshell that the MOD had not confirmed payment, even though letters had been sent for quite some time. It was hospital policy not to commence any treatment until payment had been secured. They asked if I was prepared to pay for my own operation and the additional costs. I replied no; it was up to the pen-pushers to sort out, not me. I received my injury in an IED blast, for which I was awarded for my actions. Paying for the surgery seemed a request too far in my book. They hurriedly disappeared. I'm sitting there, wondering what the hell was happening now. All my hopes of getting it sorted and being ready for the wedding had been obliterated in seconds. After a brief spell two staff entered the room to take my details and start prepping me for theatre. One informed me that Professor Wallace, the consultant who would be carrying out the surgery, had kindly put the bill on his credit card. My surgeon paid to operate on me. I was emotional; it was a kind and humane act. They then asked if it would be okay if I stayed over in a cheap hotel on my own and attended the hospital again in the morning to keep the costs down. I was in a state of shock, but after the kind gesture I agreed. I was unable to think.

Straight after the surgery I was brought round and woke up in the recovery room. I couldn't feel anything from my shoulder down and my whole left arm was paralysed, wrapped up like a mummy. A nurse handed some hotel numbers to me.

I couldn't believe what was happening. Not twenty minutes after surgery and I'm calling hotels to get a room. I didn't know if I was coming or going. All the drugs in my system, from the morphine to the anaesthetic, had me wobbling. After a while I ate some food. I somehow managed to dress myself one-handed and pack. To be honest, I just wanted to get out of there. The shame and embarrassment I felt was overwhelming. I had been reduced to a basket case.

I was waiting in the lobby for the taxi to take me to a hotel. I could see two staff looking over at me with pity on their faces. They were middle-aged ladies, most likely had kids around my age. I could tell they felt sorry for me. I couldn't look; I was grinding my teeth so goddam hard. The only thoughts racing through my head were after all I've done, all I've been through, this is how I get treated. It took every ounce of strength not to start crying. I wouldn't be broken. I'm not crying for anyone. 'Your taxi's here, sir.' 'Thanks.' Head bowed, one foot in front of the other, keep going, keep going, you'll make it to the taxi. Got in and don't remember the journey. I was numb, mentally and physically. I arrived at the hotel, booked in, got to the room. Simple and tidy. After being in the siege in Nad-e Ali and all the shitholes since, it was a palace. However, I didn't feel like a king. Completely the other end of the scale.

I got some refreshments and when morning arrived I hadn't the heart to go back to the hospital to be seen by them all over again. I went to the car park early Sunday morning, picked up my car, jumped in and drove home one-handed. My fiancée was having her hen party the same weekend. When I spoke to her I told her everything had gone well. I wasn't about to ruin her hen party with worry. A week's leave at home and then back to Chilwell.

On the Monday morning I arrived and waited for the Greek excuse for a doctor. I now think that he was just under pressure from above to sign off unwell soldiers quickly as there were plenty like me there fighting their own battles. The idiot doc still reckoned I was okay. I could barely move my elbow. I was sent to see the physiotherapist, a New Zealand man called Steve. He didn't need to do much assessing. He said I was nowhere near ready to be signed off. Thank God I had one person helping me to get better. He spoke at the case reviews and was adamant I attend the next rehabilitation course that was starting in ten days or so. It was decided, so I reported back to barracks in London and saw the chain of command about the whole debacle and the surgery as well. They just shrugged their shoulders. I was bloody raging. No support from my own regiment. I was surprised but, as you will find out in due course, it wouldn't be the only time they completely abandoned their care of duty and military covenant.

I spent a few days at home. It was the only place where it seemed that I wouldn't be getting some form of hardship. The wedding planning was again a welcome distraction. The rehabilitation course was going to be three weeks long.

Assessments, physio, education on injuries and health generally. Some exercises specific to your injuries and then tests at the end to deem your suitability and medical ranking, that is, light duties and have rehabilitation. I didn't do the tests; the physio knew I didn't have enough strength in my left arm to bang out even one push-up. He had to fight my corner all over again at the reviews. He wouldn't say so directly to me, but I knew he wasn't happy with the way I was being treated. Even he was getting annoyed that someone so obviously not ready to be given the all-clear was being reduced to this.

The day of my wedding arrived and I was still doing rehabilitation. I took a few days' leave. The wedding was great; my fiancée became my wife. She looked amazing. Most of my close pals from the military were there; the best man was my friend who had been injured in that ambush back in Nad-e Ali in 2008 during the siege. Although I had a great day, my dramas with the MOD were still lurking at the back of my mind. We all had a great piss-up. The only bit of trouble was caused by some bloke who'd been invited by a friend of my Mrs and had got pissed up. I only found out about it the next day. Another mate of mine re-educated him outside. Later that night the bloke fell out with the girl who'd asked him to accompany her; he nicked her car keys and crashed somewhere down the motorway. I was at the bar knocking back sambucas when two Old Bill walked in wearing their high-visibility jackets. I wasn't too happy about it but some others quietly got a grip of it and they left. I think I was carried over the threshold as I don't recall being able to walk. Married bliss or what! The honeymoon was put on hold until after I was finished in rehab. I certainly didn't want that on my mind then.

It was now November and I was due to start my third rehabilitation course; don't forget initially I was told by the doctor I was fine. He certainly wasn't accurate with his diagnosis. I had met some other injured lads from combat who initially were at Headley Court but had been moved to Chilwell. I'd had enough of light duties and taking crap from idiots who'd never fired a weapon in anger in their lives, but I didn't say anything. I was quite humble and carried myself and my regiment professionally during the time, although underneath it was different. I knew this would be my last course, even if I was not ready to leave. I had made my mind up if only for my own sanity. I was stronger but not up to my usual standard. I worked as hard as I could when it came to the tests; towards the end it was painful but I pushed through, beating everyone else on the course. Well, you've gotta say goodbye in style. Steve the physio gave me a glowing report on my work ethic. He knew I could have done with more time but he was stuck between a rock and a hard place. By the time I had wrapped up at Chilwell Barracks, Christmas was just around the corner. I had nearly two months of untaken leave and accrued days from being injured so I was going to be off until February 2011. Jesus, was I delighted to sign off and get the hell outta there.

After the debacle with the MOD and rehabilitation, I didn't have much time for my regiment, 21, at the time. I needed some space so I took up private security work in Iraq. So, as before, instead of unwinding and enjoying time with my family like others did, this was to be my post-operational tour leave (POTL). Previously, I'd spent it in the Brecon Beacons, training for full-time selection. Now it would be spent in Basra and the huge oilfields that surrounded it, training up local security forces and mentoring them on the mission tasks they had been allocated to fulfil. What a great way to enjoy leave, back in a war zone. Jesus, some things come naturally to an Irishman and being adventurous is one of those things.

I also had another deadline; we were expecting our first-born child in March. Another security advisor partner was also expecting. He was preparing to leave two months early to help his wife. I thought he was a lunatic. I had an idea I'd leave it as late as possible so I could enjoy more time after the birth when I'd be needed the most. I'm not too sure if I had let my wife in on the plan!

As the south of Iraq, especially Basra, has a mostly Shi'ite population, it was more secure than Baghdad and the Sunni triangle north and west of Baghdad. We maintained a low profile; our Iraqi counterparts would do the driving and most of the security detail, with ex-pat oversight. It worked better than an all ex-pat security; to the locals that would have just had invaders written all over it. Although simply being on your own with local forces can be hazardous, especially the threat of kidnap and then ransom, what would be paid for your swift return by oil companies is a lifetime's salary to most Iraqis. All you need is some of the local forces you're working with to be in on the plan and the money and you'll be lifted in an ambush. You always have to have your wits and your weapon about you. I carried US$1,000, a map, pistol, ammunition, food, water, med kit, passport, sat phone and mobile phone in what you call a 'grab bag'. If the shit hits the fan, you grab it and get as much distance between you and the threat as possible. Put a shemagh (a Middle Eastern headdress) over you or nick some local clothing to blend in and hide until darkness falls. Then go into your escape and evasion plan and training. I don't want to be on YouTube literally losing my head for those bastards; I'd put a bullet in me before capture if I thought it was the best option. That's life in conflict zones; it comes with the territory.

I was operating mainly in the vast west Qurna oilfields which were being franchised out and undergoing prospecting. The oil companies' engineers and geologists would decide where to go to look for the oil. They were hinting that this would be Iraq's second largest oilfield. It was vast flat ground; parts of it were where the marsh people once resided, when the marshes had covered up to 90 per cent of the area. Saddam Hussein had drained the marshes after the uprising by these tribes; they were later abandoned by Western governments.

My time in Iraq was now coming to an end. Fatherhood was calling and I had to make my way back out of the place and return to the UK. I arrived home with a good two weeks to spare. The little fella was born by C-section, so I stepped up to nappy duty day and night while my wife recuperated after the surgery. I enjoyed that time; it was precious. We organized support for the family. I helped my wife back to health, with one eye on her recovery and the other on the emails coming in to me. Revolution was in the air in North Africa and my skills were in huge demand. Gaddafi was losing the plot, or there was a plot against him. Time will tell. I had a brief conversation with the Mrs again at the airport, waving me off to more troubled lands. Bless her for her support; I wouldn't have done it without her. She was probably glad I was gone in some ways; men like me find it hard to settle when we're waiting for the next war zone. Now it was Benghazi or bust. Whey hey!

Chapter Eight

King of Kings

Although I'd had my eye on the Libyan situation, I had spent the last couple of weeks looking after my wife and newborn son. It was an eye-opener all right. Woah, newborn babies are tiny and fragile. We were blessed. He got into a routine quite quickly: eat, shit, sleep. Fair play to him; he had his priorities in order. I'd read a book before he was born and attended some prenatal classes with the wife. Jesus, the labour was bad enough. At one stage I was going to go for the gas to get some relief, but I thought with a room full of midwives and the missus, a man saying it was hard going for him too would have been lynched there and then. Well, the young fella was making good ground at home. The missus had healed and was back to being able to drive. I didn't just leave; I did break the news slowly and steady but, to be honest, I'd had enough of changing nappies for a while. I was looking forward to my new destination.

The reports I was receiving from colleagues already in-country were hilarious. It sounded like the Wild West, although people were dying; well, it's war. It is inevitable but the sheer lunacy of the rebels was something to behold. There was absolutely no regard for any form of military prowess; wing and a prayer was the main element of the sitreps. I had my flight details confirmed: Heathrow to Cairo, and taxi to Benghazi. I rechecked that again. Nice, I thought. I checked my maps, hard copy and soft copy. Distances, obstacles, border crossing, the notorious Salloum crossing-point at the north-west tip of Egypt near the Mediterranean. Oh, this is going to be emotional, I thought. If you've never driven or been driven on Egyptian roads, it's like they heard about speed bumps and decided, for the fun of it, to put them everywhere; although they are not speed bumps to the Egyptian road-builders, just bad laying of the asphalt. They might have been good at building pyramids but they were shit at building roads. Corruption and not giving a shit were probably the two cornerstones of the plan-and-build stages. Ah, it is what it is. So, my kit was packed and it was goodbyes once again. I set off for Heathrow and beyond. I've been going in and out of airports for a long time, especially Middle Eastern ones. I know what to pack, what to wear, what to look like and, more importantly, what not to look like, but the biggest asset when travelling in the Middle East is an Irish passport. We ain't invaded no one. I whizzed through departures; Egyptian Air it will have to do. I slept well and arrived late in the evening into a muggy, hot Cairo night. The din of the traffic was laborious while waiting for my lift outside arrivals. I knew it was *Wacky Races* time from here until I boarded the flight home, whenever the hell that was going to be!

A ramshackle taxi arrived. I gave him the hotel details. I also tipped him and spent the remainder of the drive inhaling Cairo's polluted air. The atmosphere in Cairo was toxic. Few foreign nationals walked around like before the revolution. There was an air of menace to the darkened sky over the city; people were nervous now. Women didn't venture out as much either. The hotel was a complete world away from this. I was all sorted and ready for the next stage: a sixteen to twenty-four-hour drive to Benghazi in Libya via Alexandria and the notorious Salloum border crossing at the north-west tip of Egypt near the coast. After only two hours' sleep, it was breakfast and off I went. My taxi driver spoke little to no English and I wasn't much better. I knew from previous experience we would be '*inshallah*-ing' it all the way. Oh well, when in Rome, I thought, and said '*Inshallah*' too. Jesus, we didn't go under 90 mph all the way to Alexandria. Thank God I'm a lunatic and mad driving doesn't bother me. I did ask him to settle down several times; I didn't want to fall out with him and have him leave me stranded in the middle of nowhere for him to then make out to the client I was unreasonable as I'd be out of a contract. Swings and roundabouts when you're in this game.

I could see road signs to El Alamein in Alexandria. It got me thinking about the North African campaign during the Second World War, especially when we passed Alexandria and drove west along the coast. There were many war cemeteries in immaculate condition. They stood there in silent dignity from both sides of the war. Germans, British, Italians; it was poignant. It took me back to when I was just over 12 years old. A collectable Second World War magazine was on sale in newsagents. It was issued every two weeks or so. My mum and I got it. I remember going through the articles about the North African campaign. I even hung a map of the war in North Africa in my room with all the key battles. My mum was just a girl after the war and she remembered listening on the radio to programmes on the history of the battles that had raged a few years earlier; a bit like the ones you see on the History Channel nowadays but in 1950s in the West of Ireland it was radio. I was drawn to it all; it seemed like a romantic campaign compared to the horrors of other theatres. I certainly never thought that a quarter of a century later I would be being driven in a taxi here. Even my old regiment, 21 SAS, was born out of this campaign and the North African sand. It was where the long-range desert patrol group operated a prelude to 1 and 2 SAS regiments. Wow, I thought, déjà vu. It didn't slow down Evel Knievel next to me one iota though. I looked across at him and pointed on the map to the rendezvous point where we were going to swap drivers and have a break. I pointed at the map and said 'Yes, yes?' He replied '*Inshallah*' and so did I, and I was even laughing about it.

We made the rendezvous and swapped drivers. We were on our way again; there was no change to the pedal-to-the-metal syndrome of most drivers I ever had the privilege of joining. No aircon either; the sun was well up in the sky and it was hot. Nice, I thought, I'm going to look like a tomato before I even arrive, and we went *inshallah*-ing it all the way to the border with plenty of profanities to boot with all the close calls we had. Just to explain, '*inshallah*' means 'if God wills it'. It is a common statement in Arabic, just like people in Christian countries might say 'please be to God' in the West. We suffer from 'fatalism'. We wake up in the morning, get out of bed and decide we need the toilet, but before we do we get an insurance policy set up just in case something happens to us on the way to the toilet. Fear is indoctrinated into us. Now our fatalistic Middle Eastern friends are at the other end of the scale. They don't suffer from such fear yet. Whatever will be, will be. '*Inshallah*.' So fluctuating between the two 'isms' as I do with my line of work takes some skill, nerve and lunacy at times. It's not for the faint-hearted, this craic, you know.

The Salloum border crossing comprises a few buildings in the middle of the desert between Libya and Egypt, white-painted autocratic one-storey buildings that reminded me of 1960s Egyptian films. The place was heavy with refugees stuck in no man's land, with no man's land passports. They were mostly from sub-Saharan Africa. No paperwork. Funny that you didn't exist even though you are standing there, breathing the same air as someone with a passport. Egyptians and Libyans were applying for visas. There were also UN workers, NGO staff, medics and security personnel; a virtual war zone entourage. It was hot, sweaty and there was no goddam shortage of flies everywhere. There was no queuing or getting in line either, it was a free-for-all. I paid a fixer some dollars to sort mine out fast. I got the stamps and so on. Then the crossing closed. I waited for hours to walk 800 metres to the Libyan side of the border. The taxi was staying in Egypt. Thank Christ, I thought. Eventually I crossed onto the Libyan side of the border. Same craic again. Eventually we got stamped. As I was media, I got through quicker. This part of Libya was now under 'rebel' control and their autocratic posturing meant there was zero handshaking with me. 'Ireland, Ireland,' they said, as they read my passport. I smiled and thanked them.

I was in Libya after twelve hours on the road, roughly halfway there. Eventually I met with my lift to Benghazi. Al Jazeera had sent their hired van and driver to the pick-up point. Mobile coverage was intermittent when you're *inshallah*-ing it between positions of civilization in a war zone. You have to go on your charm, wit and intuition. This driver, 'Fozy' was his name, had great English and drove steady. When we stopped for a fuel refill and coffee at a ramshackle station two hours after the crossing, I found out why he was more relaxed as he was putting the fuel into the Mercedes Vito van: fuel nozzle in one hand and a joint in the other.

I bloody roared out laughing. Jesus, if it isn't one thing it's another. Well at least I knew the drive would be chilled. When you're with indigenous forces or people in their country or land, you've just got to accept it and go with the flow. The more you try to fight it or stamp your authority, the worse it becomes. You meet in the middle over time.

We drove for another six hours or so, arriving into the mayhem that was Benghazi at about 2.00 am. After nearly twenty-four hours on the road I was shattered trying to hook up with the security team and organize rooms and so on in the melee at the hotel. I met the team leader I was replacing and had a quick heads-up. Then it was straight to bed for a few hours. The only issue was that the rebels driving around the city were enthusiastic about firing their weapons into the air, a show of ego more than anything else. They were ill-disciplined. Anyone who has ever had to practise rationing with ammunition in a conflict zone would have been appalled. I wasn't impressed; I know what it's like to make every bullet count. Just as importantly, though, what goes up must come down. The local hospitals must have been sick of the sight of injured civilians coming in from being hit by stray bullets and nowhere near the front line. There was no air conditioning and the room was stinking. Sod it, I'm too tired to care. Land of nod, here I come. There was no time to spare over the next few days; we were right in the thick of it. Straight away. Getting up to speed on the ground is not ideal, but that's just the game.

The city was awash with foreign media. NGO staff and even some foreign government officials were taking up residency at the best hotel to give some sort of legitimacy to the situation. The amount of security foreign embassy staffers had was over the top. All in their 5.11 shirts and shades; they stuck out like pink elephants. Many of these guys couldn't spell discretion, never mind practise it. The threat from pro-Gaddafi forces was high and venturing out after dark was not advisable, although the front line was now further down the coast. It would drift 50km west and then back 50km east a couple of days later. The main reason for this was that it was desert between the towns so there was no hard cover to hold; you would be flanked by the opposition unless you had depth in your defences. The rebels had held Gaddafi's forces at the city limits thanks only to NATO jets, but it was pretty hairy on the front line. Thankfully we were with Al Jazeera Arabic, so they were keen to go to the front and beyond to speak with forward observers. It reminded me of my role in Afghanistan. We were all over here *inshallah*-ing it like the Egyptian drivers; now it was from the reporter in front of the camera right down to the tea boy. If Allah will it, then so be it. As I was team leader for the task I had the uneasy task of putting some sort of structure to the whole scenario. It took a lot of work just to organize the fleet of vehicles with basic breakdown kit, fuel and supplies, med kit and so on. Sometimes they thought I was crazy for this, but it was the reason we were there, as their headquarters back in Doha, Qatar had ordered ex-Special Forces advisors to cover them and provide medical and logistical support. Money was no object to the revolution but trying to get dollars out of them to invest in breakdown kit was like prising clams open.

The front reporter was Al Jazeera Arabic's top news host and reporter in the field, Mr Beba Wald Mhade. A small gentle-spoken gentleman, he was a caring, devout man, highly intelligent and easy to work with. The only problem was his superstar status in the Arabic-speaking world; he drew more crowds than the revolutionary speakers. When Western journalists saw people flocking towards him they couldn't figure it out. You would have journalists from Europe and America interviewing another journalist. Once they figured out what was happening, there were some sour faces.

As the conflict dragged up and down the coast, moving with the tide at times, we did a lot of travel towards the east to do interviews and so on. We were in the Libyan green mountains and Derna; incidentally, plenty of the foreign jihadis fighting in Iraq and Afghanistan were from this area of Libya. Being one of only two white ex-pats among all these felt uneasy at times but as we were working for the Arabs, it seemed to be okay. We didn't mention that we had been shooting and killing their mates not so long ago. We made out we were just medics from the UK and me being Irish made it easier as well. Covering the war from the front was like trying to herd cats. The media crews would try to get as close as possible, setting up live positions with a satellite truck which would take time to set up or lower it down; not ideal when Gaddafi's forces would zero in on your position and anything up to 180mm artillery shells would rain down all over the shop. Thankfully the closest one to land didn't detonate.

Sometimes I think the military men on the other side didn't have the heart to kill fellow Libyans. I noticed this a lot in Libya. As most of Libya is Sunni they did get on well enough; the tribal divides had not yet been manipulated well enough. I wouldn't hesitate to suggest that they purposefully didn't arm the artillery shell before firing. The biggest problem about the live position is that the other side would watch the international channels, figure out where the report was being broadcast and give firing orders down the line. Hey presto. Within about fifteen minutes of a live broadcast going out, the artillery would land maybe a kilometre ahead. Trying to tell the reporter we had to go was a battle in itself. They would say it was in the distance. Keeping my temper, I'd tell them that's just the beginning; now they have eyes on us they'll correct their fire and it will advance. Lo and behold, by the time they had figured out what I was telling them was correct incoming was 500 metres and closing and then it was panic stations as we tried to get kit packed up and so on. Every bloody time. Oh *inshallah*, they will learn, I thought. Eventually the live broadcasting was prohibited by the Rebel Military

Command; at last they had figured out the benefit of not giving your position away to the enemy.

The stalemate in the east set in over the summer months of 2011. It was starting to lose traction in the news; only the big networks with the money to stay the distance covered it as the freelancers and print journalists searched for their next pay cheque in another story, in another place. They would all rush in if something big happened and then disappear again. Benghazi, the de facto capital, was tense and a political and militia hotbed under the surface. A lot of in-fighting was being passed off as Gaddafi fifth columns, but it was more the extremist and jihadi influence that we were seeing from working for an Arabic news company. Those in power in Libya, and outside, knew full well who was carrying out the fighting now.

One afternoon a few consultants and I were enjoying a coffee break from the hustle and bustle. We were located on the rooftop restaurant of the Tibesti Hotel. We were sitting chatting outside, looking over the harbour and the hotel grounds below us. As I raised my cup to take a drink, an explosion detonated below us in the car park. I didn't spill my coffee and I had been looking in the general direction of the explosion as it went off. I noticed a car bonnet had been launched into the air and the car burst into flames, along with the two cars parked either side of it. I knew there wouldn't be many casualties. The car was relatively intact, as were its neighbouring vehicles, albeit in flames. The shockwave didn't hurt us, although it did smash windows in the vicinity of the car bomb. Benghazi was not Baghdad and the sophistication and power of the IEDs in Iraq would have certainly injured us even fifteen floors up as glass and debris would have flown in all directions. I raced down to the lobby and informed other consultants to grab our clients for a head count and move away from the hotel. I quickly surveyed the situation. I sent reports to the UK and Doha confirming that all personnel were safe and accounted for. We advised plenty of people to stay away from the area as, from my experience, there are generally two devices: the first one will detonate and then when emergency services and bystanders are lured in to assist and a crowd gathers, the second detonates a short time later for maximum carnage. That didn't happen here which I quickly deduced meant that this was not the work of a Gaddafi fifth column, which is what most people were saying, but either amateur jihadis pissed off with Westerners or a rebel attempt at keeping the focus on Benghazi. Whoever it was, they were amateurish at best.

That was part of the game. Sifting the fact from fiction, as the old saying goes. Truth is the first casualty of war. The other fronts in Libya were having much better advancement. The western front was making small but steady gains in the Nafusa Mountains. The port city of Misurata, which lies about halfway between Sirte and Tripoli, had taken up the revolt in the beginning but it was surrounded by pro-Gaddafi territory. They were surrounded on three sides with water behind them.

France, 2001. My Kepi Blanc passing out parade. You certainly earn your Kepi Blanc in the Foreign Legion.

France, 2001. This was taken at one of the "Farms" where you undergo most of your basic training. Brutal, tough and violent: welcome to the Foreign Legion.

DEH Security Delta Team. Iraq, 2004. Security work in Iraq was very dangerous at this time. No insurance and no military backup meant that you literally had to shoot your way out of trouble.

Afghanistan, 2008. Many of the roads were in far poorer condition. A large number also had canals running along both sides, which were ideal for ambushing vehicle convoys.

Left: Afghanistan, summer 2008. Back to basics whilst training local forces.

Below: Afghanistan, autumn 2008. Coco was the legendary police chief from Musa Qualah and seen here are two of his policemen on a non-uniform day. They might have looked like a ragtag bunch, but they were certainly up for a fight.

Afghanistan, 2008. Close but no cigar. I was standing beside this truck when it took a direct hit from a rocket.

Afghanistan, 2008. Although not one for the usual trophy shots, the machine gunner in the photo had asked for me to pose with him. We had been fighting side by side and I respected his courage.

Afghanistan, early winter 2008. Getting some rest during the fighting. We would normally take hard cover in compounds, often staying out for weeks at a time before returning to base.

Above: Afghanistan, winter 2008. A vintage shot of an SAS man enjoying a brew before taking the day on.

Left: Afghanistan, winter 2008. Awaiting my flight details for the next battle after a sensational fighting season. Lashkar Gah, the provincial capital of Helmand province, was under attack, but I and small bunch of like-minded individuals drove straight through the lot to catch the flight.

Above: Afghanistan, 2010. What is left after our vehicle was struck by an IED (Improvised Explosive Device). The fine sand is like dust; after an explosion you can't see your hand in front of you.

Afghanistan, 2009/10. Helmand desert is a hot and hostile place. This is a typical walled compound made of mud. They are very strong and require plenty of explosives to make an impression when the need arises.

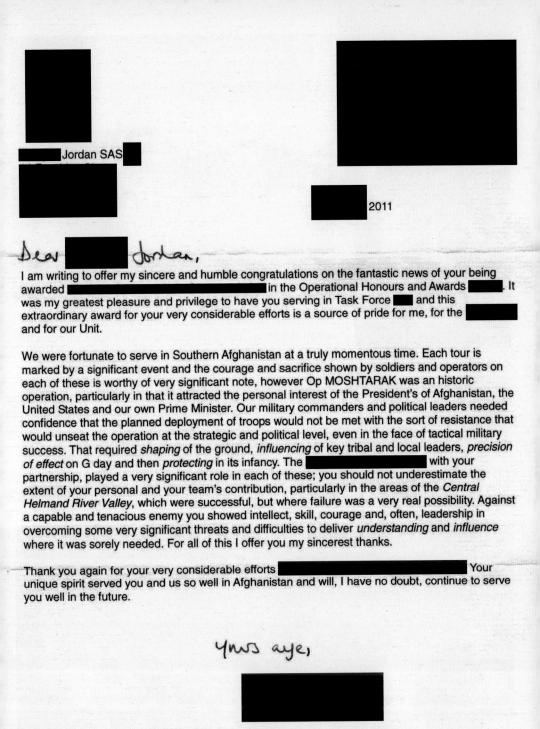

██████ Jordan SAS ██

██████ 2011

Dear ████ Jordan,

I am writing to offer my sincere and humble congratulations on the fantastic news of your being awarded ██████████████████████████ in the Operational Honours and Awards ████. It was my greatest pleasure and privilege to have you serving in Task Force ███ and this extraordinary award for your very considerable efforts is a source of pride for me, for the ████ and for our Unit.

We were fortunate to serve in Southern Afghanistan at a truly momentous time. Each tour is marked by a significant event and the courage and sacrifice shown by soldiers and operators on each of these is worthy of very significant note, however Op MOSHTARAK was an historic operation, particularly in that it attracted the personal interest of the President's of Afghanistan, the United States and our own Prime Minister. Our military commanders and political leaders needed confidence that the planned deployment of troops would not be met with the sort of resistance that would unseat the operation at the strategic and political level, even in the face of tactical military success. That required *shaping* of the ground, *influencing* of key tribal and local leaders, *precision of effect* on G day and then *protecting* in its infancy. The ██████████████ with your partnership, played a very significant role in each of these; you should not underestimate the extent of your personal and your team's contribution, particularly in the areas of the *Central Helmand River Valley*, which were successful, but where failure was a very real possibility. Against a capable and tenacious enemy you showed intellect, skill, courage and, often, leadership in overcoming some very significant threats and difficulties to deliver *understanding* and *influence* where it was sorely needed. For all of this I offer you my sincerest thanks.

Thank you again for your very considerable efforts ██████████████████ Your unique spirit served you and us so well in Afghanistan and will, I have no doubt, continue to serve you well in the future.

Yrs aye,

██████████

This letter is what I held on to the most when I was in hell with illness. After all, those that had failed to help me included my own regiment. This simple thank you helped keep me going. I knew I would make it. I just had to remember the real me.

Libya, 2011. Gaddafi's huge residence and military barracks at Bab al-azizia, Tripoli. He famously gave a speech from this building, to which NATO replied with air strikes.

Iraq, winter 2010/2011. Training and mentoring local forces, just outside Basra in Southern Iraq.

Libya, 2011. Sirte, Gaddafi's home town, was the last city of the regime to fall. It was surrounded on three sides by rebels and the Mediterranean Sea to the rear. The amount of ordinance dropped here really showed the hatred amongst the different militia towards Gaddafi forces.

Libya, 2011. Booty from the spoils of war. Trying to get armed militias to hand over their weapons to the Libyan government was one sticking point. Soviet era tanks was a whole other debacle.

Libya, 2012. This trophy of war used to reside with the Libyan Air Force in Tripoli. It was liberated by rebels from Zintan, in the Nafusa mountains, Western Libya, where it now calls home.

Libya, 2012. Zintan, in the Nafusa mountains. The Zintan militia had an impressive stockpile of weaponry. These tanks were used to defeat Gadaffi forces all the way to Tripoli.

Libya, 2012. Leptis Magna. An hour east along the coast from Tripoli. This world heritage site is vast, with much of the site still not fully uncovered and is one of the most magnificent examples of the Roman empire outside of Italy. Here you can see the real Libya and all of its history, culture and people, not some inter-tribal divide that has been exploited to ruin a great country.

They had to fight to survive. The port remained open, although intermittently. Al Jazeera Arabic had a news crew in place. One of the consultants in my team was also there helping them. That was a shitty place to be during the early months of the siege, but once they managed to push the artillery back enough so that it was out of range of the city centre, life was more bearable. I would organize the logistics for the crew in Misurata and get them on board a ferry that was operating now as a refugee and medical evacuation vessel out of Misurata to Benghazi. I would also brief the incoming Arabic reporters and crew on the situation, give them basic medical lessons in first aid and so on, and brief them on some dos and don'ts in life-threatening scenarios; give them some memory aids that would kick in when they were in the middle of an artillery barrage. It was just the basics in life-saving techniques and then we'd send them on their merry – or seasick – way to the besieged city via the Mediterranean. Being at the quayside when the ferry would come in on its return journey was bittersweet: all those refugees, and the young men with missing limbs and so on from the war making their way back here and then on to Turkey for medical treatment. It was a solemn sight coming down the gangplank. Different war, same outcome.

The stalemate on the eastern front made my work easier though, as we got into a routine which worked well; we were able to implement some training and so forth during down time. It certainly helped that I could get a better night's sleep as I wasn't up all hours prepping for long stints out of Benghazi. Yet conflict zones never stay the same for long. There was a lot of bustle around the Al Jazeera Arabic Bureau in Benghazi. They were getting initial reports that one of the top military commanders for the rebels had been arrested; General Younis, an ex-Gaddafi-regime general, had defected. He was said to have been a close ally of Gaddafi at one time. I knew this would make life hectic again. The rebel factions were barely held together and this arrest could be a catalyst for it to get very intense, not just around the front line but back in Benghazi.

Our base at the Tibesti Hotel was where all the media worked and stayed. Most press conferences were held there; it was very high-profile but it was well protected. Also media types like to be around media types, get an inside line on a story and so on. When it was announced Younis was dead… wow! The place erupted not long after that. I was ushering some of our staff away from the firefight that was ensuing outside. I even had to brave the bullets a few times like the good old days just to run out and retrieve some who were frozen to the spot. The reports from the National Transitional Council (NTC) were that an armed gang had killed him. I had it on good account, only a day after the Tibesti assault, that he had been executed alongside two of his aides-de-camp. Another young officer had sneaked into the boot on the way up to Benghazi. General Younis and the two loyal officers were shot by the 17th February Brigade. The young officer reported the story to Al

Jazeera Arabic. He was stowed out of Libya to save his life. The story was quashed. It didn't look too good, NATO planes giving close air support to al-Qaeda. The jihadis had had their revenge or they had been ordered by their paymasters to take him out. He was about to blow the lid on who exactly was now fighting the war in the east. I knew Benghazi was a tinderbox. I just hoped it wouldn't catch. It was a long way to safety if it did go tits up.

I was looking forward to getting back to the UK soon. I was due to fly in a few weeks. Also Ramadan was now in full swing. Our Arabic clients wanted to do some news pieces on the front line and beyond that to where the rebel forward observers were hiding so they could call in the artillery on the Gaddafi forces front line; they also acted as an early warning for any movement towards their own front lines. We travelled most of the day on dirt tracks and off road, going past different defensive rebel lines. Eventually we were right at the front now during Ramadan. A Muslim must fast between sunrise and sunset. No smoking and so on. A lot practise it; the only problem is that about 6 to 8.00 pm local time is when most people are at their weakest, including their patience. That's when arguments start. Here I was, the only Westerner among rebels of all descriptions; most were practising fasting, but plenty of others weren't and were smoking cigarettes. One young rebel offered me a fag. I was gasping; I hadn't had one all day. The minute I lit up, we were opened upon with 150-220mm artillery shells; the bang they made going over our heads. They were landing 2km behind where we were all laying up. The Arabic reporter smiled and said at least they're not that accurate. We watched the impact areas of the shells hitting. 'No,' I said, 'you see where they are blowing to bits over there, that's our only way out of this area.' The vehicle couldn't navigate the surrounding steep terrain. He stopped smiling. '*Inshallah*; it will be fine,' I replied, laughing. I had become well used to that saying by now.

I was due to fly out of Cairo within a week. I needed a holiday. Something was afoot though; Al Jazeera Arabic were busy. They had been given a heads-up from Doha that an offensive on Tripoli was looking likely to break the stalemate, and it looked certain that they would be moving with the front or travelling via ship. A road move was too dangerous at the time as half the country was still in pro-government hands. My task was ending soon.

A day before I was due to go home, an email arrived. I was asked if I was interested in travelling to Tunis and rendezvousing with some National Public Radio (NPR) journalists to assist them in covertly entering western Libya and on to Tripoli for the battle for the capital. I couldn't resist; once more into the fray. I apologized to the wife and did the dreaded Benghazi to Cairo suicide drive. After the flight to Tunis I had some down time waiting for flights so I had quite a few drinks in the hotel. It was one night out; I needed it after months in war. It was sheer lunacy at Tunis Airport. The number of media journalists trying to catch a flight to Djerba in Tunisia near the north-east border with Libya. Every man and his dog! I managed to catch a flight on standby and arrived late that evening, exhausted; just over twenty-four hours of hurling myself across the whole North African continental coast. I'd be going like the hammers of hell to make this task work. The deadline was to be there for the fall of Tripoli and that was looming ever closer. I met up with the clients and sneaked them across the border, all the way to Tripoli. We found their work colleagues and managed to get a room in the Radisson Hotel in Tripoli. No food or water. Well, there was a war on. We'd had the foresight to stock our vehicle to the roof: a robust red Toyota Hiace taxi van; not my usual choice but very apt and it fitted in at all the checkpoints and so on. No one batted an eyelid.

I went to my room, opened the door and saw it was occupied, that is, someone had left their belongings in there but they weren't in. In a lot of hotels, not just in Tripoli, but where there is any civil unrest or war that breaks out fast, people leave stuff behind and try to get out of the country in a hurry, catch the last flights and so forth. The same thing looked to have happened here. I had a quick look about; I noticed a fine collection of cravats lying on the dresser; ah, must be an Englishman at least. I did some further detective work: I was like one of the three bears trying to find out who's been sleeping in my bed, except it wasn't Goldilocks, it was John Simpson of the BBC. I knew the Beeb hadn't left Tripoli, so I left my kit in the room and went to search for the BBC's head of security, an ex-22 man. We squared it anyway. I made sure the room was intact, got another room and duly moved my kit to it. I did it out of professional conduct. I later spoke with Mr Simpson who thanked me.

Tripoli had fierce fighting all around the Gaddafi compound. All the various militia wanted to have the battle honour. The amount of stray ammunition flying towards the hotel was a concern. Bullets were going through windows all the time. We were a few kilometres from the battle. It subsided over a few days. The capital had heated exchanges in some parts. I was busy looking after a team of about six clients advising and helping in logistics and so on. I had taken the role on the promise someone would replace me after a few weeks. I had a family holiday booked and paid for. My replacement arrived, a good friend and colleague. I handed over everything to him at the Libyan/Tunisian border. 'Cheers mate,' I said, 'I'm off for two weeks in Italy.'

No word of a lie, I was wrecked now. I would sleep like a baby. Oh, Tuscany was immense. My wife, young son and me. It was as far as you could get from conflict zones, or so I thought. Under my skin something was eating away at me. Initially I put it down to tiredness; my arm had not healed as well as I had hoped. The insubstantial treatment by the MOD and my regiment failing in its duty of care were making me angry and resentful. I buried it in a few sessions on holiday but now, looking back, that's where I made my first mistake: ignoring what was under the surface and just getting on with it; that's all I ever knew. To make matters worse, while home I received a very kind letter from the officer commanding the unit I had been attached to in Afghanistan during 2009/10, congratulating me on being awarded for my actions in that year's honours and awards list. I was touched and proud and very humble, but there wasn't a dicky bird out of the administration staff or notice from 21. That didn't help with my situation. I thought fuck you, if that's the support you show soldiers when they come to you for help. Bitterness was starting to grow.

More wine in Italy sweetened me up for now. After Italy, I had relaxation time at home in Hertfordshire. I'd been home about a month when the telephone rang: an offer to be team leader for Al Jazeera English in Tripoli. Wow, I thought, I wonder if they're anything like their Arabic counterparts. I soon figured out that was just a culture thing. Flights confirmed; I was off again. Libya via Tunisia, road move to Tripoli and a lot more of the same driving experience. Tripoli had been taken by the rebels in August and the fighting was in Sirte, Gaddafi's home ground. Bani Walid, an hour's drive south of Tripoli, was still loyal and contesting the conflict; a lot of tribes were making their mark.

It was now mid-October. The role was more of the same, to try to provide organization and clarity to the clients in Doha. The news teams had allocated advisors and were doing their news-chasing. I just had to chase the chasers and so forth. It worked well. I also had a reporter in the capital and I would advise him and his crew when they would be out news-hunting. The news filtered through that Gaddafi had been caught and killed. Al Jazeera English led the news across the globe. I was in the main square with one of Al Jazeera's top reporters, James Bay, a tall Englishman with a hearty laugh, a real gentleman. He and his cameraman were surrounded by thousands of celebrating Libyans. It was a hectic day keeping the live positions going and free from over-enthusiastic crowds but it worked.

After that Tripoli and most of Libya fell quiet for a while. Everyone was unsure what would happen next. We set up a news bureau in the capital, and for the next couple of months reported on the political and every so often the various militia in-fighting that was part of the course. Yet as the east started to disintegrate even further and with serious in-fighting in the government of the day which had no real mandate or power, it was evident that armed militia from all over Libya still wielded the gun and power. Libya wasn't a beacon of revolution any more. It didn't look good on the news now. So, no news is good news. Al Jazeera English wrapped up the bureau in Tripoli. They were more interested in Syria now. I had enjoyed my time with all the various reporters and crews for the different media outlets during the Libyan revolution/conflict/coup. Journalists, camera crews, photographers and support staff work tirelessly and are professional in making the deadline or that live feed. Paragons if somewhat foolhardy at times, but hats off, they bring us what we want to see from our sofas and they're in the middle of it making the sacrifice. Also it was summertime in the UK and now I had an additional member of the family: a baby girl. I couldn't wait to get home but for how long I wasn't sure.

Chapter Nine

A Dark Night in Benghazi

Home life was also hectic. I hadn't noticed but it was brought to my attention that I seemed distant to my family. When I was back in the UK I would engage with family life but I did take time away, mainly to go the pub; not big social sessions, just a quiet boozer to read a broadsheet for a few hours in peace. In the back of my mind I was angry, and the bitterness was growing about the state of my upper arm. I had tried some rehabilitation on my own but since the arm wouldn't extend fully, I had muscle wastage in the top part, bicep and triceps. What made it worse was the guilt I felt about it. I would replay certain events from Afghanistan over and over again in my mind. It may sound unusual to some, but part of me thought I'd have been better off more seriously injured. Maybe I would have been treated better. I had been blown up three times, and lost count of all the other close calls with bullets and the like.

Yet what ate away at me was could I have done more to help those who didn't make it or those who were more severely injured than I was? I felt a sense of shame of where I was at. I really didn't know what was going on or how to deal with it. I didn't even know where to start in tackling the issue. The solution I came up with, like many men, was to go on the piss and bury it under the mantra, 'Man the fuck up.' The seeds of destruction had been well and truly sown. I thought that throwing myself into more work would be the answer, that the issue was only that I had time to think. It would pass. The anger didn't, so I contacted a few solicitors to sound out a case against the MOD for medical negligence and failure of duty of care. I instructed one solicitor to start putting a case together. I thought to myself, if nobody wants to help me I'll do it myself. I stood up and was counted on many occasions; I'm not having these bastards get away with it.

A work colleague from Libya called. Was I interested in assisting a media team covertly entering Syria? I said I'd speak to him face to face. I gave an initial yes, but I did have reservations about Syria. I was well up to speed on it from colleagues and journalists that I had contact with. I also went through a lot of reports on it. I knew work may head in that direction so best to be up to speed. My associate and I met up. I received a comprehensive breakdown of the task. I said yes. There'd be two security advisors with medical training assigned to a two-man media team: a cameraman and a reporter. We would be entering Syria from the Lebanese side of the region. Jesus, I thought, they'll love an Irishman in Beirut. The flights were confirmed. Fly from Heathrow into Beirut. The main issue with Beirut is that it's a hotbed for foreign intelligence services and has very impressive electronic warfare capabilities, so there's all the other intel stations working there. No phone. Best option, little or no emails. Keep as low a profile as possible. We stayed close to the hotel, only venturing out to recce certain routes and so on. We were waiting for the fixer, that is, the person who is a go-between with local services and so forth. They usually know most of the dodgy and the non-dodgy people, and speak Arabic and English as well as the local dialect. The other advisor had been in a few times and had a stake in the company I was working for. He and the fixer did a lot of the reconnaissance and organizing. I did med training, sorting kit, maps and so on.

When we finally got the go-ahead and the smugglers were in place I would be travelling north to Tripoli and then on to the north-east to the Lebanese village of al-Qasr. From there, it would be across the mountains on foot, into Homs province in Syria and make our way through the smuggling chain into the town of al-Qasr several kilometres inside the border.

All along the Lebanese border is a military zone and only locals and military get past the checkpoints. No foreign nationals are allowed inside this area. There are military checkpoints on all the mountainous roads. We would be stopping and walking up into the hills to wait to meet with a middleman, who would then take us to a safe house and then another would take us to the border to be passed on to the next link in the chain. There were a lot of unknowns. High risk wasn't close to it, especially with the fact that Westerners were a commodity in a place ravaged by war and the capture of us by anyone was a real threat as they could cash us in and hand us over to more extreme elements in Syria. It was turning into a bit of a joke; we were circumnavigating the checkpoints and the road below, as we were in the hills above, but our smuggler was lost, even though the road and car lights could be seen only 400 metres below us. He took out his phone and the whole area where we were was illuminated by the backlight. Now I had serious concerns. This guy had never done this before. You could tell he had just been asked or set up to do it. It was a 3km trek handrailing the road a couple of hundred metres up in the hills until we passed the checkpoints and got into vehicles on the other side. We did eventually make it to the safe house in the middle of the night. We got our heads down while one kept watch. It was early morning; it was hot and there were plenty of flies. The plan was to lay up all day until darkness and then make the next leg of our journey to the border and get passed on. As the day went on it became abundantly clear that all the time on recce, the fixers and the other security advisor I was working alongside had decided not to go the professional smuggler way. They'd set the whole thing up themselves. The smuggling fees for entering Syria were big bucks and the media companies would willingly pay. They'd decided to set it up and cream the vast majority between the fixer, the consultant and a few Mickey Mouse locals.

On the other side of the border were contacts in the Free Syrian Army, a very nice name for a militia. They would be carrying out most of the escorting and logistics from safe house to safe house. They would get some money but they were doing it for the 'cause', not the money. So my two associates clicked on to this, just organizing it themselves and pocketing the money.

It was late afternoon and some of the family members involved in the safe house where we were staying, near the border, started arguing among themselves. Others wanted a cut of the money being made by our host. After a while we received incoming small-arms firing from some neighbouring houses. I thought, we're not even in Syria yet and this is what's happening. Our cover was blown by greed and by being amateurs. Not long after, a Lebanese military officer stopped his vehicle outside the house and spoke with the owner either about the gunfire or someone had spoken to the military about foreigners trying to cross into Syria. It didn't matter; they knew we were in the area and would be patrolling on the lookout for us. More importantly, so would others on the other side of the border in Syria, either pro-Assad forces or other groups. We were walking cash cows to the local impoverished people. They would get the equivalent of a year's wages for us. I spoke with the fixer and my co-advisor; I didn't trust them either. Well, I said, they had made the decision for us. It was stupid to go forward as all our cover was blown. The best thing was to lay over until darkness and get back down to Beirut as quickly as possible, before we were thrown into a Lebanese cell for a few months as a warning to other media trying to use the Lebanese routes. We were successful in getting back to Beirut. Our four days up in the northern mountains were over as soon as they'd begun, but I was pleased.

I had my departure flight confirmed. Sweet, out of this cauldron. We were supposed to be going out on the town for a few drinks with the media crew. I had my kit packed. I politely declined going on the piss. I hadn't the stomach to sit there and be fake, smiling. I knew what had happened and I didn't want to be around it. The news reporter telephoned me, inviting me to join them. I made my excuses and went to bed. I had worked with him in Libya and I was pissed at the way they were treating him and the cameraman. We all like to earn a few quid on top, especially when it's with a big media company, but being this greedy and putting lives in more danger than they already were when going into Syria was just shameful, particularly the fact that they'd put their own lives in greater danger for being so short-sighted. Just ask the relatives of the journalists captured in 2012 around the same time and same area. You do not fuck about in war zones.

I was back in Blighty and I promised myself I wouldn't work with people I hadn't worked with before or had reservations about. Ah well, at least the Olympics were on in London; that would do for entertainment. I took up residency in the local boozer during the afternoons. It was the only peace and quiet I was getting or, more accurately, thought I was getting. I had been chasing up the solicitors and filling out forms and statements. The next stumbling block was getting my military medical records released. The usual shite is even worse if you're a Special Forces soldier; any excuse not to help. It was just adding to the anger boiling up inside me. The wife and I were not getting on. I was cold at times and never around. I would pay for a helper with the kids and the housework but I wouldn't be there, and if I was I wouldn't talk about much, I'd just watch telly and complain about the injustice of austerity and so on. This negativity was growing inside me.

I buried the resentment and other issues deep inside me. I didn't realize at the time that what I was doing was the worst way to deal with it, but I didn't know any better and I didn't actually think there had been any issues. I was fine; it was others that had done wrong to me. The Afghan part of the equation I buried also. I just couldn't work that out either.

The summer in the south-east of England was a big buzz, with the weather and the Olympic gold fever; that took my mind off it and I enjoyed the time with the family. Then I received an urgent call asking how quickly I could get to Heathrow. 'Hour and a half from now,' I said. I always had a holdall packed, ready to go. I had been on short notice ready for contract work for a considerable time. The only items to add were clothing that was hanging up to prevent creases. I received another call within minutes: 'Get to Chiswick west London with your passport.' I needed a visa sorted to fly with the client, CBS News. I arrived within the hour, handed my passport over and collected some medical kit and body armour from the company I was contracted to. On my return to the CBS News London bureau I was made aware of the task and the urgency of it. The passports would not be ready until the morning so I returned home and awaited confirmation. All sorted. I would meet with the cameraman and receive my passport and visa at Heathrow. I'm well used to rush affairs and making deadlines by the skin of your teeth. It's not that I don't plan ahead; if you work within the media field, especially in conflict zones, it's all reactionary and you're chasing the story to stay ahead of the pack. That's why they call it exclusive. The US Consulate building was attacked on 11 September 2012 and there were dead and injured in Benghazi in Libya. I was frantically getting the cameraman and the camera kit through Tripoli customs to try to get an internal Libyan Airways flight over to Benghazi.

There may have been a change of regime but the customs bureaucracy was still the same. To be fair, the amount of camera and editing kit we had in cases was a lot for just one cameraman. He said better to have it and not need it than need it and not have it. I've used this phrase plenty at times so I was on side. Customs, however, were on the other side. I called a British Airways local Libyan representative I had befriended on a previous trip. I knew the man would come in handy in the future. Fair play to the British Airways rep, he squared the whole thing like magic. The next hurdle was to try to get on a tin can with propellers. I used my extensive Irish charm on two Libyan Airlines ticket-desk saleswomen. Oh, being Irish is a godsend at times. After some fluttering of their eyelashes, hey presto, two tickets appeared on a flight that was already full. We must have taken up half the hold with our kit alone. The plane was vibrating and the pilot hadn't even switched the engine on; people were sweating and shaking and that was just the trolley-dollies. Jesus, I wasn't sure if we would make it to the end of the runway, never mind to Benghazi. The man across the aisle smiled. '*Inshallah*,' he said and so did I and I bloody well meant it.

I was laughing as we roared down the runway; this thing was about to disintegrate with the vibration. Overhead compartments opening, people praying and I was gritting my teeth: stay goddam airborne. I was preparing myself to be jumping out of a plane, except I had no parachute this time. Sod it, I thought, airborne all the way so up, up and away. We landed at Benghazi; the landing was all right. Soon as it landed the vibrating went berserk again. I didn't care now; we were ahead of the news pack. No time to waste: through the airport to a waiting van and straight to the Tibesti Hotel, Benghazi. This place had been like a home away from home over the last eighteen months or so.

Surprisingly the hotel was quiet and there weren't as many Westerners frequenting it as usual, neither media-, NGO- nor oil industry-related. Even out and about in Benghazi itself it was quieter. Women with headscarves or full burkas were more prevalent than ever before. The one other giveaway was that I didn't see nearly half as many women drivers as before. Even Gaddafi, despite his madness, was a liberal in a lot of ways. The city had a dark feel to it but not all was lost. The younger generation were still on the internet; they hadn't given up on their revolutionary values. I met up with the rest of the news team, Charlie D'Agata and Agnes, the producer. We went straight to the US Consulate compound to go over the scene. We were the first Westerners at the Consulate building and over the next few days we would be the only ones. As soon as we arrived, suspiciously, eastern Libya airspace was closed down. That slowed any other journalists attempting to arrive. The buildings and area inside the walled compound were still warm from the fires started during the attack. The local Libyan guards and police were friendly. I don't think anyone high up in Libya or beyond, especially in Washington DC, expected such a substantial and detailed journalist coverage and investigation from our team.

As I was the only military man with experience on the ground, I pieced together much of the attack. Most of the facts were verified by witnesses we found and interviewed. We even found the separate building that was to be called the Annex, on which much of the news and darker side of the attack was concentrated. My detective work started to pay off big-time. When I searched the Annex and the surrounding area, I put together the weapons used in the attack. We even identified that the place was a CIA black ops site; not from paperwork or anything, just good old-fashioned experience in war. Everything I put together for CBS News was reluctantly admitted to by the US State Department, after previous denials. It wasn't only the US Consulate that was a mess; it was the whole set-up, the security procedures, the rescue mission, but most of all – for me painstakingly walking those grounds and the roof of the Annex where two US security men gave their lives protecting the US civilian staff hunkering down below them in the building – the carnage of blood, medical supplies and spent ammunition on the rooftop. They'd been calling for help using a technique I've seen used by Special Forces worldwide; it's basic but it works. I thought to myself, here is the might of the US military and these men were reduced to the basics to survive. Whatever they were trying to communicate to in the sky over Benghazi that fateful night, it abandoned them in their darkest hour, that much was evident. It reminded me of many of the tight corners I had been in over the years. Same story: good men fighting for their lives and to save lives while the machine does bugger all to assist.

I was proud of my contribution to that news story. I certainly did those men who died proud by making sure the world knew how they held on and fought with courage beyond duty, and how they were abandoned. The rescue from Benghazi in the early morning was also haphazard. I'm not criticizing the people carrying out the role; they did what they could with the time, information and tools at their disposal and that is the crux of it, the tools at their disposal. The might of the US military and the rescuers were having to scrape together a local militia to assist them: the February 17th Brigade again; recall that lot from General Younis's death. That's why the whole debacle was shrouded in mystery and denial. Various US security, political agencies and so on were protecting their own interests and there was no communication from Secretary of State Hillary Clinton. It was an exercise in arse-covering.

A few days later, I even spoke with some members of the February 17th Brigade who had been part of the rescue team that went to the consulate and then constructed an outer perimeter cordon well outside the Annex. The attack came from within the cordon itself, from the only high building overlooking the CIA Annex. As soon as I went onto the roof I figured that out. How the attackers managed to get inside the cordon is one thing, but not to be apprehended after launching the mortars and rocket into the building? It would have been visible for all to see. Unless, and it's a strong possibility, the February 17th Brigade, who were under CIA mentorship, turned on their paymasters, as they had the best available opportunity to run US forces out of Benghazi and let the east of Libya descend into jihadi and extremist control. It wasn't Cameron who lost the plot; it was the Yanks themselves back in 2012. CBS News genuinely did an excellent job on reporting the worst attack since 9/11 on US soil. We interviewed many suspects and even had ice cream and juice with the supposed ringleader. It really was the most bizarre event I've seen in some time.

Charlie D'Agata had been replaced by Liz Palmer, another charming reporter. I was impressed; she had these so-called extremist leaders under her spell. They would not go on camera, but they openly talked about the protest aspect of the attack and were walking around Benghazi without a care in the world. Even members of the police came into question for the inadequate response. I figured a lot of it out, but I declined to release my conclusions to the news team without concrete evidence. Yet I knew this was not just the work of some fevered-up extremist wannabe warlords. The accuracy of the Annex attack was impressive. I even said it was very accurate, even by Western forces' standards, especially with the fact that there was no evidence of corrective fire with the mortars and so on. They hit it first time. That means the kit used to determine distance, elevation and so forth most likely had infrared capability. This is all high-end and not what the fighters in the back of a Toyota pick-up have in their fighting order. The whole affair stank of a pre-planned and pre-emptive attack on the US. The worst thing is that there were most likely people in the know in the US that knew it was going to happen and they let it happen; for what purpose, who knows.

We returned to the UK and only a few weeks later I received a call to go back and assist CBS News again. I did. There'd been a mini-revolution in Benghazi but the dark side was back in control. We spent a few days on the story again, as there were hearings in the US Senate about the attack. The official US investigation never really did much in Benghazi. It seemed no one was interested in stirring up trouble in Washington over the deaths of a few of their citizens and the evacuation of their staff. It was like Vietnam all over again; another mess.

I was glad to be finished on that task. I knew it was over in Libya. The place was on the verge of full-scale conflict again between these armed militia or extremists. It was going to be very unsafe for Westerners for the foreseeable future. Also, no one wanted to report on the sham revolution and what a mess it had descended into, otherwise all the people eating their dinner back in the West might start asking questions about the whole Middle East, like Afghanistan, Iraq, Syria and Libya; all that I had witnessed had a common thread. The innocent civilians pay the heaviest price for the greed of the power-hungry and the few. These people deserve so much more. The hospitality and warmth I received in all these areas from many, many people showed that we are all the same underneath. Same loves, same fears, same hopes, irrespective of creed, colour or anything else. We should look for our similarities, not our differences.

Chapter Ten

Combat-Stressed

Life in Hertfordshire was not rosy by any stretch of the imagination. My wife and I were not on the best of terms. We had two young children and I was barely there. When I was there, I felt so unattached to life, even though it was all around me. I had what most people dream of: a beautiful home, family, an interesting career. It all looked well on the outside but scratch under the surface and it was the complete opposite for me. My marriage was in trouble; working away, never mind anything else, was putting it under severe strain. I was self-medicating on alcohol to hide the torment building inside me. A dark cloud had descended over me and all I could muster to deal with it was escape. The MOD litigation was slow and continuously bringing out bitterness in me. The Afghan memories just played over and over again. Some days it was like I was literally being blown up time and time again. The guilt I felt and shame. 'Man the fuck up' was my rallying cry and I got it from the wife enough as well. I hadn't a clue what to do about it. I just isolated myself from everyone and everything. My sleep was erratic; I kept trying to fix myself by planning the future, the next job, the next something, and not dealing with the present. When I kept busy, it was a distraction. I thought keep going, keep going, no matter what. That the soldiering on attitude would get me through.

So when a phone call came from an old friend about a potential career in a natural resource exploration company in Afghanistan – steady work and so on – I thought this was the answer to my prayers. I genuinely believed this would solve my problems. I really was naive about the extent of the treatment I needed. To be fair, I didn't even recognize that I was ill at the time. You can't fix something if you are not aware of the problem. It was probably clear to some people, but to me it was just life and it wasn't me who had the problem, it was others. I was going to be in Kabul and then it would be on to the north of Afghanistan over the Christmas period, while many ex-pats were on holiday. There was the option of taking up a full-time role as a training officer within the company. It was the news I had been waiting for. At last I could have a steady career. Although it was still working in war zones, I still to this day enjoy that line of work. I am very good at it. I would know when I would have to leave and so on. I could start to plan for the future, with my family. I was selling this to myself and my wife as the solution. Sadly I didn't know what the real problem was, never mind a solution.

I got busy straight away studying and researching everything I needed to know about the role. I confirmed flights and booked the hotel in Dubai while I was waiting to obtain an Afghanistan visa. I couldn't wait to go, although I would be missing my daughter's first Christmas. I was looking to the future; the present was what I was avoiding. I left for Dubai from Heathrow. Finally, I thought, I'm going to get some good luck. I arrived in Dubai, obtained the visa and went to the hotel to await a night flight from Dubai into Kabul, Afghanistan. I don't know what happened in those few hours but I decided to have a few drinks before leaving. It was the stupidest idea ever. Once I got a little intoxicated it opened up my mind and I just got really drunk. Looking back now and recollecting that moment in my life, I realize I was very ill at the time; my inner spirit was telling me not to go on, to stop and to find out what was wrong underneath the façade, but I couldn't do it. I just buried my pain in drink.

Of course I missed the flight and I spent a few days drinking myself into oblivion in Dubai. The bars are full of ex-pat veterans coming and going between war zones, all with the same credentials. Phone was off; no emails. I had vanished. People were concerned, both in the UK and in Afghanistan. When I eventually sorted my head out, I made up a cock-and-bull story about airport security going through my bags and arresting me for no reason. It happened a lot in that airport. They hated Western security guys. I made my way back to the UK in time for Christmas. I had fucked myself properly with that debacle. I had lied to everyone about it. I really didn't like myself. Now I didn't know what to do. I received a call from the company I was supposed to be starting work for. They asked if I was still interested in an interview in the New Year in Mayfair, London. I thought God was looking out for me, giving me a second chance. Wow, I was in complete denial about what had just happened in Dubai.

Christmas passed and the New Year too. I really don't remember it, as my mind was full. I attended the interview and continued with my bullshit airport arrest story to cover myself and my illness, which I really didn't recognize in me at that time. The interview panel was impressive with some former officers with great military careers behind them. They were impressed with my experience and character. I was chuffed when they went through my résumé and commented that I had done a lot for my time. Looking back, that should have been a sign to me. These exceptional men, who had reached the pinnacle in their endeavours, thought I had done a lot. I needed a time-out but that wasn't part of my DNA then. When I found out I had been successful in gaining employment I was ecstatic once again. I was planning the future without a care about the present moment or what had just happened in Dubai. I was ashamed of my actions and of lying to people and my peers, but that is one of the symptoms of illness and the denial of the illness or ignorance of it and how it manifests itself in your life. The one person

I was really lying to was myself. I do not give myself a hard time about it. I was sick and I was unaware of it. I didn't mislead people before I was ill and after the correct diagnosis and treatment I don't now either. Honesty is probably one of the biggest factors in my recovery.

I blocked out what I needed to. I returned to Kabul in the New Year as the training officer for a Kabul-based mining exploration company that had huge expansion plans for Afghanistan. I knew my role would be demanding and high-pressured. I relished the challenge. I had risen to similar challenges in the past.

It was the start of January 2013 and Kabul and most of the northern half of Afghanistan was in mid-winter snow. Wow, was it cold. The company I was working for had two villas in central Kabul's diplomatic quarter. Kabul's security situation was quiet enough, with only the occasional explosion and gunfight. The winter snow needed to melt to free the passes for the spring offensive. I settled in quickly and my role began to expand rapidly. I would be responsible for the setting-up of a training area for future static guard forces at the potential exploration sites, as well as training the Kabul security details on their static and mobile security operations. All the security for the natural resource company was to be carried out in-house. It made sense; we were all ex-military and a lot of the Afghan security working for the company were also ex-military. Although the experience varied widely, trying to implement a coherent system of training and protocol after it had been ad hoc for some time was very difficult, particularly when it came to changing the Afghan culture on work ethics.

I would spend most of my days organizing and planning for this training camp north of Kabul and then it would be further north into two provinces that were nearly two days' drive in opposite directions in the mountains north, where roads existed only in one's imagination. I relished the work and I was starting to relish drinking after work in the evening. I never used to drink when I was working away. Now it was commonplace. Communication with the family back in the UK was difficult. It was all starting to seriously get on top of me now. If I wasn't working I was in my room isolating myself and drinking to hide the turmoil in my head. The day job and my deteriorating health were at loggerheads. Part of me wanted to speak up and say I needed help; the other part of me was screaming at myself, don't say anything; if you do, that's you finished. The shame, ignorance and stigma of it drove me to drink and to hide what I was going through. In actual fact, unbeknown to me at the time, I was inadvertently making my illness worse. If we deny our sickness, then we deny our treatment. You can't have one without the other.

I ploughed on regardless. Targets and dates fast approached. I was on top of it but barely. One slight unknown factor would have put my timelines off, but this was Afghanistan. This was still a war zone and the logistics of the operation were to be an incredible feat in itself, with the organizing of hundreds of men, transporting them around remote Afghanistan and setting up training facilities too. This was high stakes, high rewards for anyone to be dealing with, never mind an unwell veteran. I really was beginning to get snowed under as the drinking was getting toxic. This was the strongest symptom that something was awry with me. I had a few days' break in Istanbul to sort out visas for Afghanistan for the long term. I really didn't want to go back and I was also scared to speak up. Hindsight is twenty-twenty vision. When you learn you're ill and the exact cause of the symptoms and the treatment available it is a huge relief, but when you're in the middle of what can only be described as turmoil within your head, your capability to make rational decisions for your own wellbeing is reduced. Plain and simple, if you don't know about it, you can't fix it.

Well, whether I liked it or not, it came to a head back in Kabul. I got into a drunken fight in a club and that was that. It was obvious to all now that something was wrong. I received the news from the in-country manager that my services were no longer required. I do think I parted on good terms with them, as they knew it was for personal reasons and they had made a recommendation to me to speak to some professionals when I returned to the UK. They also gave me a generous remuneration to assist while I was home. I was relieved that I was beginning to understand what had been happening with me. Don't get me wrong, I was still in pain and feeling shame for what had happened. I felt like I had let everyone down. Not everyone knew about the incident. I disclosed it to a few trusted friends. I didn't know what was next but I knew I needed help and I started to research post-traumatic stress disorder, PTSD. I also took myself to a mutual aid group to assist me in stopping my alcohol intake. I knew that it was a severe stumbling-block to getting well. I didn't think I had a problem; I just thought I needed to be sober for a while.

I decided to stabilize myself for a while, keep out of the pub and establish a routine home life. I didn't want to push the PTSD issue to the surface. I was scared that the stigma and so-called loss of face would be a disaster for my career, even though it was a disaster already, but when you're stuck in the eye of the storm it looks calm. I was just hoping it would change or that I could turn it around. I was hoping that the external factors would make me better on the inside. I was in complete denial. I didn't want to recognize what was happening. Although most of the symptoms were playing out in my head, not drinking was having a positive impact on my family life with me being more reliable. In hindsight, I was only white-knuckling my recovery. I hadn't put any form of treatment in place. Basically I was holding on, hoping I wouldn't get any worse without getting any medical treatment for my illness.

That white-knuckling lasted about two months. My family was away visiting relatives and I stayed at home. I started drinking again and everything resurfaced straight away. It was the final straw for my wife. She telephoned to inform me she and the children would not be returning to the marital home. I didn't believe her, but as the days passed it became clear she was serious. I was numb now; I realized what the hell was going on with my life. I was in shock. I just couldn't figure out how I had ended up here. It was like I was in a nightmare or living in a parallel universe. I hadn't a goddam clue what was going on around me. I thought I must have been a right bastard in a previous life to have all this happening to me. In hindsight it was ignorance about the illness, its symptoms and what treatment, places and people were available to assist in recovery. I honestly thought it was me versus the world. I did manage to steady the ship somewhat but with no family at home, all I had was an empty house and a head full of memories.

I received an urgent call. A client needed a consultant with an Irish passport. It was an unusual request and they added could I fly to Dhaka, Bangladesh within a few hours. Of course, the usual reply. I always had everything ready. Just add some crisp, ironed clothes to the luggage and that was that. More details started coming in about the task ahead. The client was Primark and they, with quite a few other UK clothing brands, had garments being manufactured in a textile factory in Bangladesh. The Rana Plaza factory disaster is what emerged from the collapse of an eight-storey garment factory in Savar just outside Dhaka, Bangladesh. The initial outlook was not good for the occupants of the building; the images flashing on the news showed a severe building collapse where most likely thousands had been working away moments before disaster struck. I would be accompanying one of Primark's directors, Katherine Kirk. My role was security and advising on logistics, assessing their offices and so on, and advising their local staff on the dos and don'ts. In all, it was essentially to keep a low profile. This disaster was being used as a huge political tool within the Bangladeshi political scene. Furthermore, a lot of international textile brands were not owning up to the fact that they were using the factory to supply them. Basically Primark took their responsibility seriously from the outset, and from what I could observe on the ground in Dhaka, they were immediately putting in place short-term and long-term strategies and rolling them out to help the victims' families and survivors.

I assessed the situation and advised that it was necessary to maintain a low profile for the Primark staff in Dhaka; it would simply be cheap news to shove a camera in their faces and bombard members of staff with questions that they possibly couldn't know the answers to so early on in the disaster. I felt now as I did then that some UK brands were pushing certain media outlets to keep the attention focused on Primark so they could catch up or avoid their responsibilities. That's the nature of most corporate companies. I was proud that Primark, with a vast expanse of its UK customers from the working classes, was standing up and doing what was needed to be done; not for the cameras or for sales but simply because they actually cared about their role and their stakeholders, from the customer to the maker of the garments. Even before the disaster, Primark had a lot of ethical practices in place in South-East Asia. They were a shining light to all other companies involved in the sector, many of which wanted to join in the disaster relief efforts but remain out of the limelight.

The first few days after the initial collapse were heart-breaking. The number of fatalities and injured kept rising and personal stories were coming in from local charities that Primark had partnered with before the disaster as part of their ethics programme and which were now were stepping up logistics and finance and so forth to meet the escalating situation. There were plenty of tears from the many staff affected by the disaster. I sure was glad to have been there to assist at that time. A lot of my experience from war zones, particularly casualties and rehabilitation timescales and so on, was well-utilized. We did the rounds at the various international charities and agencies that are involved in Bangladesh. I was able to put all on hold and concentrate on the task. I think, for me, I could identify with a lot of those involved in the disaster. My heart certainly went out to them. It felt good that I was in a position to be able to help. I relished the work. I admired Katherine Kirk for her steadfast professionalism, and although it hurt with all the media garbage, she was more concerned about putting together a concise and concrete programme to assist those affected. She was not interested in soundbites for television. I remember observing her in a meeting and thinking to myself I could learn a lot from this lady; what she has brought to the table cannot be underestimated. I think of all the Western people involved in the aftermath. She led by example. I was impressed.

We were to have a short break back in the UK and I would then join another team who would be taking up where Katherine had left off while she reported to the board and so on. The final days in Dhaka were still busy but as the death toll climbed and the extent of loss and rehabilitation became known, the political landscape changed. Now both political parties were using the collapse for their advantage. There were strikes and foreign fingers were always in the pie as well. I didn't comment on it; I had seen it all before. Some of the long-term strategies Primark were putting in place were going to be impressive. I was asked if I was interested in joining the team. I was glad to be thought of in that regard and duly said yes. This would be rewarding work but demanding. It certainly felt like the right thing to do.

As we arrived in Heathrow and said our goodbyes, I returned home. I dropped off the bags and out I went; I didn't return for a few days. I was back to square one all over again. When I eventually mustered up the courage to sit in my own house, the full extent of the car crash that was my home life hit me. It hadn't done so before, but coming back from Bangladesh to the emptiness in the house and the emptiness inside me ruptured something. I couldn't sleep and in the early hours of the morning I just snapped. I couldn't take it any more. I was lying in bed, shaking, sweating and my head racing at 100 mph. Do it, just do it, I kept saying over and over in my head. I started to imagine that life for my family and friends would be better if I wasn't around any more. At that moment in time I made the decision to kill myself. I thought that it would end the torment and the nightmare that all this had become. I genuinely thought that suicide was the best option for everyone involved. I sold the idea to myself that I was doing this for others to be happy.

I grabbed the bedside lamp and ripped the electric cable out of the lamp. I went to the upstairs landing where the wooden banister uprights are, the handrail part on the landing. I checked the wooden uprights to see if they would take my weight. I knew that when a person was hanged, they mainly kick out, have heart attacks and shit themselves. It's the body doing everything it can to get out of dying. I didn't want anyone finding me dead and covered in shit. Also, I didn't want the neighbours hearing my last death kicks in case they would come to my aid. I wrapped the cable around the wooden uprights at the strongest point, wrapped the cable around my neck and tied it off. It didn't have the height for me to swing from it, but I wanted to lower myself slowly to check that the wooden upright would take most of my weight. I did it slowly. I could feel myself getting drowsy. When you're that close to death there is a real calmness about you. I had no thoughts in my head; I wasn't crying. I lowered myself further. Some spiritual teachings say that when death is very close the calmness that transcends you is another portal opening up. I didn't know it at the time. I just thought I was doing the best thing for all. I was now losing consciousness almost as though I was just falling asleep. I don't know how long I was unconscious; all I remember is darkness and an image of my two children at the centre of my vision. I was definitely unconscious, and yet this image was sent to me; it appeared where your third eye is, just above your eyes in the centre of the forehead. It was a quick flash of about three to five seconds. It brought me to sharply. I didn't know what had just happened, but as I came round I knew I didn't want to do it now. It took me at least thirty minutes of wrangling and pulling to get out. I barely had any oxygen but I wanted to live.

Eventually I freed myself. I lay there shaking, a blubbering wreck. I lay down and just held on for hope. I was screwed and broken. After a lifetime of war zones, of being blown up three times, rocketed, mortared to shit, thousands of bullets whizzing past me at close range or ricocheting off items near me, I couldn't grasp that it was me that nearly killed me. I thank the heavens to this day for sending me that image of my children. I call my kids my guardian angels. The universe, God, call it what you like, deemed that I had more to give in this life. At the time I didn't know or comprehend that. I was now teetering on the abyss. When you are that vulnerable it only takes a slight knock to send you down into the next layer of hell. I had dropped into a few by this point.

Thankfully with hindsight I came to see that this was not the answer. If you're thinking of taking this route out, trust me, your head and the voice in your head will tell you anything to make it sound like the only solution. It's not a solution. It's the problem. The wreckage you leave behind is not worth contemplating. Because if you die, you kill your loved ones too. It's just that they die more slowly. No matter what happens, hold on, just bloody well hold on. Get your head on to that pillow and tomorrow is a new day.

So here I was, lying on the floor, lost and numb. I telephoned a helpline and spoke with someone, or at least tried to talk. Words would barely budge off my tongue. I was that cut up. I think I just wanted to hear another human voice. I didn't want to feel alone. As the morning passed I came to, and in usual fashion tried to bury it and just carry on. One foot in front of the other. Still thinking that the answer would come from the future or the next thing. I let the clients know that I was struggling with the break-up of my marriage and they made the sensible decision to leave me back in the UK. I also made the decision to stay in the UK. I would look for work that would have me home every evening; well, that's what I thought. The truth was that with my illness I wanted to isolate myself and not have to show my face.

Within a few weeks I was self-medicating on alcohol and drugs just to stay awake at night and not to face life or the cold reality of the situation. I had made contact with Combat Stress, a military charity that had rebranded itself during the Iraq and Afghanistan campaigns. Everyone seemed to think they were the leaders in the field. I was awaiting assessment by one of their outreach team members. Between their somewhat poor administrative practices and my illness, this seemed to drag on through the summer. I made contact with the charity on several occasions to enquire about where I was in the process of being seen. Finally, in October of 2013, some five months after initially contacting them, an ex-military officer, who was now employed with a military charity – that is really a private medical business masquerading as a charity most likely for tax and other purposes – got in touch. We met near to where I was working in Central London. I told him my story and answered his questions. I also informed him that I was struggling to stay in work as I could barely do a couple of days at a time. The period between the cycles of depression, anxiety and everything else was getting shorter and shorter. I was on a waiting list to be seen by a psychologist at London Veterans' Service in Camden, North London. I was hopeful that perhaps I was getting on the right track now. When I went for the assessment, it was difficult. I tried to be honest and open up, but I still had this belief inside me that I was a failure and that this issue was not worthy of me being a man. It really rips at the heart of my identity, although I was mistaken in this belief.

At the time, for most men, and women I think as well, especially if you have been used to that kind of life, having to face up to the illness is the biggest stumbling-block. This has more to do with stigma and misconceptions about these health issues. The interview went okay but when I received the assessment which was written up and posted to me and my GP, I wasn't impressed. They seemed to pretend that they were listening, but then they put their opinion on it and that's what it is, an opinion. Half the questionnaires I filled out were put together by pharmaceutical companies to build their drug-dealing business. I was given the wrong diagnosis and coupled with that it was Christmas 2013 and I was all alone. I couldn't go back to Ireland. They didn't know what to do either. I was an Irishman who had been in the British army; to top that I was ex-Special Forces. Nobody knew, well I didn't ever tell anyone even about being ex-military. So trying to recuperate or get help in Ireland was out of the question.

No family, and I had isolated myself from my friends. I was a prisoner in my own mind. In the attempt to cope I now had substance and alcohol addiction to boot as well as the PTSD and other issues. Jesus, I was on fire: sleep-deprived, relentless paranoia, flashbacks and nightmares (when I could remember them). Being in a chemically-induced oblivion on a daily basis was my way of dealing with it. I was begging for a place on a six-week programme at Combat Stress. It would be six weeks before I could access any treatment. I did the interviews with the health professionals and got clean and ready for the rehabilitation course which was due to begin in March 2014. It was the only good news I had in twelve months, that maybe I might be on the mend. I had everything to hope for. My bags were packed and train ticket ready. I locked the door of the house, and thought to myself next time I'm here I'll be in a much better place.

Chapter Eleven

Prisoner of War

It was a mild March Sunday morning. I travelled by train to London and back out to Leatherhead in Surrey to give me a day to settle in before I'd start the course at Tyrwhitt House, the south-east part of Ex-Services Mental Welfare Society that has been assisting ex-service personnel since 1919.

It had now been sexed up and rebranded as 'Combat Stress', another casualty of the Blair Witch Project. I was hopeful that their help would lead to an improvement in my circumstances. I was physically and mentally drained. It was coming up to a year since my family had left. The summer and winter of 2013/14 had taken a ferocious toll on my wellbeing. I so wanted this to be the cure I needed, just to stop the pain and the burning in my head and body. Non-visible injuries may build in the mind but boy, do they manifest in the body. The effects of the chemicals being released by the brain and the substance addiction as well disrupt your whole system. How I had made it this far was a miracle in itself.

I presented my cert and was shown to my room. I would have the usual tests carried out by a nurse. Heart, blood pressure and so on, and then I'd need to fill out some questionnaires and get assessed on my present mindset. It was being run like the military and that was comforting, although the staff were all civilians. The hierarchy at the top table that we patients don't see are ex-military officers, with some whose careers had been in mental health in the military. The usual shit: when they'd been in a position to do something about it, they hadn't bothered. Now they'd migrate over to military charities and old allegiances, and the old boys' network would come into play. I didn't have this attitude when I walked through the gate. I was here for rehabilitation, no more, no less. The assessments went okay; they were just being cautious and ascertaining if you were prone to being violent or suicidal. I assured them not today anyway. I still had a sense of humour. You damn well need it at times like that. I had a scout around the place and met a few more inmates; it didn't take long to assess what's what and who's who.

As with all institutions there were political, rival factions and so on: disinformation and some sick bastards. I didn't want to get wrapped up in any shit. I chatted and had the craic with lads, usual exchanges. When they asked what regiment you were in, that normally changed the conversation. I was going to be with these lads in rehab, attending workshops, classes, group therapy and taking food together for six weeks. I told them 21 SAS and left it at that. I never get pulled into speaking about my military history, training or ops. What you read here is a basic description. I don't big-time it. I don't have to. Those who are arrogant think they are good; those who are assured know they are good. Plus I didn't want this taking anything away from my recovery. I just wanted to be part of the programme and fit in and get on with getting better. Sleep was very poor, with the new environment and a lot on my mind, the latter being the understatement of the century. We all got our various cohorts/groups and weekly timetable, and found out which individual key workers, psychologist and psychiatrist had been allocated to us. I was a wreck, but I was hopeful.

I settled into the routine straight away. The familiarity of the military life and having the veterans under one roof was good. There was a real camaraderie among the lads, always is. My therapist would not be at work for the first full week of my programme. I wasn't happy and it slowed me down, but I engaged with the other classes and workshops. In the second week I was introduced to my therapist and it was like talking to an ice cube with legs. Not too sure where they pick these people from, but I would have thought that people skills and communication skills, being able to get a patient to open up, would be a basic prerequisite for employment. I was hitting a brick wall here. I only wanted to build a rapport; I was in no place to discuss anything. I didn't even trust her yet. It was like they were all reading from a script. The arrogance was astonishing too. I wasn't completely closed-minded to rehabilitation. I thoroughly enjoyed the mindfulness and the craft workshops. I also found I had a knack with poetry. This was like a whole new avenue through which to express myself. In the classes we would read out poetry from literature given to us. The lady leading the class would always ask for our understanding of the poem and so on. I could read well between the lines. I had a canny intuition for seeing what the poem could mean at several levels.

However, I was becoming acutely aware of a two-tier system operating in the background. Those who dared to speak out or question any of the lessons given by the psychologists and therapists were marked. Not everyone attending was on the six-week course; many were older veterans who had been attending for years when it was still Ex-Services Mental Welfare Society over the door. They warned a lot of us about the high turnover of staff; good people leaving or being pushed out. It was obvious this place was being turned into a factory. I didn't like what I saw, but I told myself that I was here to get my life back on track and with that I made the decision to ask for a change of therapist as the ice cube on legs showed no sign of even pursuing the thought that she was human, never mind conversing with another one. I had hit an impasse and I thought this was the sensible option. That request was ignored. On a Thursday during week three they said my key worker would have a meeting with the therapist to sort it out. What they were not prepared to do was have someone think for themselves. They only wanted injured veterans that would take to the programme. Out of each cohort about 20 to 25 per cent seemed to be doing okay. The rest of us, and we all were experiencing different levels of illness and treatment, didn't like what we were being taught. They were trying to programme or brainwash us just so we looked good enough at interviews. If you didn't agree or were not ready or whatever, then they had you marked as non-compliant.

What really upset me and many others was that we were being treated as stupid squaddies that could be treated like children, and those with university degrees and initials after their name knew better. When you put your hand up that you need help for non-visible injuries, you lose your right to self-defence; you may be ill but you don't suffer from stupidity. Your word, even your character, can be called into question and these so-called medical professionals hold the keys to your freedom. That threat was exercised over many in that place. Don't get me wrong, there were plenty of decent staff doing their best, but they were not in control.

My attempt to get a new therapist went on for several more days and in the end there was a complete breakdown in communication with the therapist. I was summoned to a meeting between my psychologist, the treatment centre manager, my psychiatrist and a head nurse. I went in and spoke clearly and concisely. I had been asking for a change of therapist for nearly a week. They just wanted to break my will and get me to jump through hoops. I was threatened with the police by the head nurse. I only asked to see my medical records. I retorted, 'You ring the police and I will telephone the *Sun* newspaper about this place.' That silenced them in shock. The meeting was abandoned. I came out. I was on the verge of breaking down, but I wasn't going down without a fight. I telephoned an old sergeant from 21 SAS. I told him the story and the way they were mistreating me. I said it's immoral and illegal and violated countless medical ethics. He advised me not to sign any paperwork and not to budge; he would contact the regimental welfare officer for 21 SAS. Finally, I thought, some help from my regiment. I informed the staff I had spoken to my old regiment and I was awaiting a call back from the RWO (Regimental Welfare Officer). That put the shits up them. They knew now that their underhand tactics were going to be blown. One of the staff who had been in the first meeting decided to call another one. They informed me that it would be sorted out in the morning and to just rest.

Rest? I was so stressed and at the end of my tether. How the hell had it come to this? Trying to kick me out of treatment because I said it wasn't working and I needed a change of therapist so I could open up and get on with getting better? It's not rocket science. I got a phone call from my old sergeant that evening telling me to stay put and keep my head down. They would get to the bottom of it. It felt good to have some back-up after nearly four years on my own since the screw-up with my arm and after having asked for help then. The next morning I was informed there would be another meeting around midday. I said fine. I asked if I could continue the workshops; that was a negative. Midday came and another meeting. This time they brought in another consultant psychiatrist to take over my case. They wouldn't swap a therapist, but when it suited them they swapped my psychiatrist because the other member of staff had felt shameful about the way I was being bullied and screwed over. I recorded the whole thing on my phone as evidence. They didn't like it, but I know the real reason they wouldn't show me my medical records; they would fill in bullshit after they got rid of me. That's why I wanted the meeting to be recorded so I could contest it. Otherwise it would be these bastards' word against a sick veteran. What chance did I have? They tried their best. I said I was waiting for the RWO to get back and whatever would be would be. The slimy bastards were trying to put words into my mouth. Half of them hadn't the courage to look me in the eye. I looked straight at them:

> I've seen too many good men blown to bits or shot to shit to roll over and play dead. If you think you're going to break me and get me to sign off that I wasn't engaging in treatment, think again. I swear before God and anyone else I will not be beaten or broken. I will get to the bottom of what's going on here and the way you are treating veterans.

Much pain has passed since that day and that statement but, my friends, I'm damn well back in the ring. To those who carried out that act of treachery and betrayal towards me and the other veterans and who I witnessed making names for yourselves and money off the backs of our suffering: screw you and thank you. It was my damnation into a burning layer of hell for nearly two years after that. Yet when I said I'd make it back, I meant it. I really meant it.

Okay, back to the shit-storm meeting again. So that one was abandoned. I spoke with the RWO and he said to remain there and he would see what was going on. I informed them I had spoken to him and I was awaiting his move. They asked me to sign a consent form so they could speak to the RWO about me directly. The head nurse was a tall, skinny string of piss with no backbone. Every ounce of me wanted to knock the bastard out, but I wanted treatment more than anything else. I played it cool. He put a blank A4 piece of paper in front of me. I responded: 'You're telling me, an organisation like Combat Stress that talks and communicates with many agencies about patients, that you don't have a data-protection form or a blank consent form template?' Goddam idiot just walked away. The RWO telephoned. I gave him a heads-up and told him what had just happened and that I had not given permission to anyone to discuss my case. I wanted this made as official as possible. I wanted this torture to be recorded and dealt with through the proper procedures. The string-of-piss nurse came out again. I said no and went to my room.

It was evening time by now and I was a nervous wreck but I didn't give it away. There was a knock on the door at about 7.00 pm and the Treatment Centre Manager was standing there with a letter; she smirked and said good evening. I didn't like her smirk; I knew something had put the ball in their court. I read the letter that said they would be discharging me at 10.00 am and I would sign my release form and so on, be discharged and look at coming back for a check-up. You get discharged and then they cover their arses by giving you a follow-up appointment. They knew full well nobody was going to come back after being treated like that. Then it would go on record that the patient didn't engage in treatment. I telephoned the RWO. No answer. He was supposed to call back that evening. I left a voicemail. Later, it rang out and I left another voicemail. A while later I tried again; this time it was switched off. They had contacted him without my express permission and that was that. They lied and convinced my regiment that the best thing for this sick veteran would be to stop his treatment, and the regiment, which I had twice asked for assistance, did not even bother to answer the phone. I couldn't believe it. Sodding all on my own again, the whole system against me. No wonder that bitch at the door had a smirk on her face. I sat on the bed and cried.

How could it have come to this? I had lost my career, my family, my sanity; lost all that I hold dear to me. I wanted to get better and to try to get my life back on track. Now there was nothing but the darkness of the night. The thought of going into the office again and having those bastards sit there and hand me a paper to sign myself out… no bloody chance, I thought. I may be screwed but I ain't dead and they ain't going to beat me or laugh and wave me off as if it's a game to them. I packed my kit. The night staff did their evening round at 9.00 pm. I was in my room. They couldn't see the bag or anything else. I said hi and told them I was chilling in bed. Once the coast was clear, I got out my bag and hid it under a bush in the gardens. I made my way back into the television area to see some other lads. I didn't say what was going on. I just wanted some camaraderie before I left into the darkness. The night staff had seen me so I knew no one would check until morning. With that I went to my room, checked for the all-clear, sneaked out the window through the gardens and put my hold-all over my shoulder. It was dark and cold; it was the end of March 2014. I kept low, sneaking through the woods on the grounds. I scaled the fence and headed into the woodland surrounding Leatherhead in Surrey.

I marched a solemn march. Teeth gritted, but with the stride of a man who wouldn't give in. I handrailed the road until I could make out the town's lights. I edged down the road, avoiding cars, until I made it to the train station. My head was covered and my eyeballs were to the floor. I changed my top and so on before going in front of the CCTV and the station. I wanted to be missing so it would be official at Combat Stress, and then it would come to light what had happened to me and I thought it may stop it happening week in, week out. I made my way to Central London and on out to Hertfordshire.

I turned up at my front door and I remembered the thought I'd had: that I would be in a better place on my return. I dropped the bags and went straight to the off-licence. I got a supply to last a while. I had no intention of leaving the house. I had no idea what had happened over the last forty-eight hours, but I felt like my liberty was at stake here. Those bastards could get me sectioned just for the hell of it. I wasn't going to give anyone any excuse. Plus, I wanted me missing for it to be official. No sleep that night. Around 10.00 am I got a call. I didn't answer; I knew it was Combat Stress. I had the number saved on the phone. They didn't even leave a voicemail. I texted one of the lads still inside and asked if they had been looking for me. He said no, they were keeping it quiet and a few lads were asking questions and not happy about what had happened but the staff were saying sod all.

Later that morning the phone rang again and no answer. The staff left no voicemail. I contacted my estranged wife and told her what had happened and not to worry, that I was okay. I wasn't happy, but I was okay. It must have been surreal for her to hear what had happened, but I assured her I didn't do anything wrong and I would keep her up to speed over the next few days as I would call to speak to the kids. She was listed as my next of kin. They never contacted her either. So it was well over eighteen hours since they had seen me, but no contact with the next of kin. They rang my number but again, left no voicemail. They knew I had attempted suicide before and that I wasn't happy about what had happened. I hadn't been suicidal since that image of my two children had saved my life; I'd had thoughts, but that was all. I wouldn't be going anywhere.

Eventually at about 5.00 pm there was a knock at the door. I opened the window upstairs to check who it was; it was a local police officer. He said they had received a phone call from Combat Stress and that I wasn't happy about my discharge. I didn't make a fuss and said I was okay. He could see the pain in my eyes and he didn't pursue it. He asked if I was okay; I said I was. I knew what he meant. They had reported the attempted suicide and that I was a vulnerable veteran. He was assured of my safety and that was that. I thought shit; now I'm on the radar everywhere. One little side step and they have the ammunition. I dare not leave the house for a while, especially during daylight. The darkness was now my only companion. Quite literally the darkness of the night and the darkness within my soul and mind. What have they done to me, I thought. The Taliban didn't do half as much damage as the very institution and agencies that are supposed to be there for us. How I would like to bring to light those at Tyrwhitt House who had tried so miserably to break my spirit, from the treatment centre's management to the psychologists, psychiatrists and head nurses.

They should bow their heads in shame. To be honest, I don't know what was more traumatic, being blown up or being exploited, bullied and harassed. When your mind is so fragile and you've lost so much, to have so-called health professionals who are supposedly employed to help you write up sodding notes on my medical records to sully my good name was an ordeal too far. After being awarded for my service, I was subjected to threats by cowards. Yet I would also like to thank them for what they did to me. That drove me on to get better; their methods weren't the most orthodox, but they worked in the long run.

The next several months were one long battle in hell. Day was night; night was day. I had completely fallen into alcohol and drug addiction. Anything to stay awake at night. It was a vicious spiral in only one direction, downwards. I couldn't leave the house most of the time; only on occasions. Everything had to be delivered; even torment comes straight to your door. The odd time I would be so pissed off at being a prisoner in my own house I would be high as a kite and go out. Those excursions ended up in fights or in a police cell. Fair play, the Old Bill didn't give me a hard time. I had spoken to a civilian while at Combat Stress; he worked alongside the police. He informed me that blokes like us have to be careful; even if we used self-defence against a few attackers we can get done for it. He read out the code this falls under with the police, so they know they're dealing with a trained killer before they come running onto the scene. That kept me good and paranoid half the time. I tried not to give anyone an excuse to take my liberty, but the reality was that my illness was denying me my liberty.

Being isolated for weeks and weeks on end before I could see my kids was slowly killing me and my spirit. After a visit from the kids it was even worse. I just went into oblivion; it was the only way I knew how to cope. Christmas 2014 was a painful, lonely experience. The only thing I liked about that time of year was that it was dark early, and when it was the daytime the light was crisp and bright. I could get out more during the darkness but that was a double-edged sword. The night-time was longer and my head would rage or fear in equal measure. It was early into the New Year. Well, I wasn't paying any bills now. After the systemic abuses with the financial crisis, I thought fuck you, it's your mess, I'm not paying to get you bankers out of it; plus I was broke. Inevitably the letter from the mortgage company arrived. Repossession proceedings were going to be starting soon. I cared, but at the same time I didn't. Losing the house would be the final nail, I thought. All would be lost. My mind and body were running on thought alone. I barely ate and I was very ill and vulnerable. The paranoia was frightening. I really didn't know what was in my mind and what was real.

I contacted the Royal British Legion for assistance with the house. I knew I was too fragile to fight this alone. The debt advisor, a Welsh lady called Lyndsey, was brilliant, although we were only delaying the inevitable. I was hoping that my

Armed Forces Compensation Scheme (AFCS) money would be paid within the next weeks to months. I didn't know the amount, but I was certain it would clear the arrears and buy time to either sell or get better treatment. I had started to see a private medical professional to begin dealing with my illness. I was nowhere near ready to start talking though; I was still traumatized from my treatment at Combat Stress. I contacted the Veterans Agency about an update on my claim. I was told it was on hold due to issues arising from the injury to my arm and that it was being revisited to see if the amount was correct or whether it was to be increased. So the PTSD was on hold while a separate claim from my 2010 injury was still being sorted. The AFCS is a slow, miserable torment that screws injured men left, right and centre. As bad as it is, it's worse for war veterans before 2005. They get even goddam less. It really is shameful the way we are treated and swept under the carpet. The military covenant is a worthless piece of propaganda for the dispatch box.

There should really be a full and independent judicial inquiry into the treatment of veterans and injured veterans in this country. Things have not changed much since the Spanish Armada in 1588 when injured men from the battle came home. It was only charity and some ships' captains that paid compensation or helped in some way. Even then it was nowhere near what was needed. So do your own homework. Every monumental war and battle that has been celebrated over the last 500 years paints the same story. There is no bullshit, it's just hidden from view; it doesn't go down well for those basking in the glory to retreat on the real cost or the abhorrent treatment of those who sacrificed so much. Anyway, now you know.

Getting back to where I was at, the ruthlessness with any illness of the mind is that it is a parasitic illness. It manifests in every part of your life. I was coupled to the drug and alcohol addiction that stemmed from the illness of the mind. Self-medicating on drink and drugs is one of the biggest issues faced by veterans and hinders treatment as it makes non-visible injury far harder to detect, with many seen as just having drink or drug problems. I was chained to a never-ending groundhog day over and over again. I tried to pull myself out of it, to make steps in the right direction, but I'd fall down again or descend even further into a hell of despair that I couldn't escape, even though I had made countless efforts. I was all alone, although I now know I was in people's prayers and thoughts. The Royal British Legion were there, my family tried to assist in any way they could from Ireland, my former wife did what she could, but the nearest person in my close circle was 200 miles away. My illness had isolated me in a cell that was my home. Now that was about to be ripped away as well. That was knocking lumps out of my fragile mind.

By March 2015 I had been diagnosed with psychosis from a breakdown from the mistreatment the year previous and all the changes in my circumstances had taken their toll. I was on very strong medication. I tried to put in some sort of stable regime for medicating myself but after a while it started to become abundantly clear that I was just sitting on the sofa staring into space dribbling. The television was on but I couldn't concentrate on the movement and flickering; my eyes were sore from the hypervigilance and little to no sleep and so on. It felt as if my soul was being consumed in front of me. To make matters worse, the repossession hearings came and went. Looking back it was a godsend that I was given a few adjournments while I waited for the AFCS to ascertain exactly what I was going to be paid. I was basically pissing in the wind when the final hearing arrived and I got the news that I had a few weeks to have something in concrete by June, otherwise eviction proceedings would commence. The magistrates and the mortgage company were both as lenient as they could be. I was grateful for that. I can't thank the Royal British Legion enough for helping me out. I was glad it was all over now. My head and heart were not in it.

In a way I was glad the house was gone; it was killing me inside. I felt like a prisoner. I donated much of my belongings to charity; I had no place to put them. Then I made the decision to move north to Yorkshire to be closer to my kids. Only seeing them every six to eight weeks was not helping me or my kids. I thought to myself, the only thing I have is my kids. Since my home was now gone, what had I left to lose, eh? I also foolishly thought that a lot of my problems would dissipate if I moved somewhere else or new, but all the issues were inside me. So no matter where you go, unless you deal with what's going on inside you, the same problems just reappear. You may change things on the outside, but until you change what's happening on the inside it's the same old story again and again. The definition of insanity: doing the same thing over and over again and expecting different results every time. Jesus, this hindsight is great value for money, but when you're busy in the middle of the storm it ain't so pretty.

I moved north, staying with family until I found a place of my own. I knew I had made the right decision. My little guardian angels were in great form and just getting to see them more started to pick me up. I tried to sort out the substance abuse addiction by having a few pints. That theory sank many a man. I didn't know anyone about; my mind was still very ill. It didn't take too long to find somewhere to live and start isolating myself and feeling my illness again. As the winter drew in, the nights closed in too and I realized the darkness in my mind hadn't disappeared. It had lulled me into a false sense of security. The paranoia was severe by this stage. I made a few attempts to try to get help and first start working at detoxing. Every time it would get worse. In October I had been through a period where things were starting to work. After a few days I found a twelve-step meeting. I decided I needed some help to keep this going. I went to a meeting at 7.30 in the morning. Here were people who had lost everything, had never had anything to lose or were just normal and had been to the pits of hell and back. They had a glow about them though. My mind still had its grip on me and it took me further into hell.

The next six months were the worst in matters of the mind. I had lost all else but this was a new hell. Most mornings, after doing the night-watchman until dawn, consisted of being knocked out from exhaustion. Over and over the same shit, but the intensity was now of tectonic proportions. I would spend half the day in a fantasy that I would get better, beat the drugs and alcohol and start to get better. Put weight on. Start looking after myself. Then, as the day progressed, the paranoia would unfold. I would literally spend hours in the crouched position either staring at the door or in the direction of the tiniest creak in the house or sound outside. If somebody walked past the house the sound of their footsteps was like a Roman legion going into battle. I would barely breathe so as not to give away my position. There wasn't a sinner around, not even a mouse. My adrenaline and heart rate were at maximum for a minimum of eight hours every day.

Christmas came and went. All alone again, though I did manage to see the kids when I was able to get it together enough to see them. In the New Year it was the same shit, but occasionally I was managing the odd day here and maybe two days there without the substance abuse. I kept trying every day. I was caught in a fantasy about sorting my life out, followed by the paranoia and guard duty at night. Then a few circumstances presented themselves: a break in the darkness, literally. There was a spell of great weather for springtime, the clocks went forward and suddenly the night shift shortened and there was light. Most mornings I would beg for help in ending this nightmare. Squeezing my eyes shut tight, I'd hope for peace and freedom. Absolutely shattered, I asked for help. I don't know who I was talking to but on 1 April 2016 I did the exact same routine and asked, help me, help me. I can't do it any more. I'm screwed, I'm screwed, I'm beaten. I can't go on any more like this. Someone please sodding help me. I fell into a deep sleep. I woke that evening. Something got me into the shower and I managed to eat some food. I was weak but I kept going. I made my way to a twelve-step meeting. I was shaking and rattling. I didn't know what was going on. I couldn't speak and couldn't look anyone in the eye, but something underneath had changed.

Chapter Twelve

Surrender

Looking back, it definitely seems like the universe, or whatever you want to call it, had a sense of humour. April Fool's Day is when I awoke. When I got home that night from a mutual aid group I really didn't know what was going on. The only thing I knew was that I didn't want to use alcohol or drugs to deal with my illness. I didn't sleep much that night; my head was a mess. I was detoxing and sweating and shaking. I didn't care. I thought at least the shit is getting out of my body. Frankly I knew I couldn't control my life or my illness. I surrendered to the fact that I was powerless over the addiction and I would not ever be able to control it or even get healthy again without first tackling the drugs and the drink. What started as a way of dealing with the illness became an illness in itself. I knew something had definitely changed, but I hadn't a clue what it was and I wasn't about to rock the boat trying to find out.

I kept busy. That weekend I attended more mutual aid meetings. I knew the answer to addiction was inside those rooms and I knew dealing with the addiction would lead me to dealing with the PTSD. I couldn't fight the two enemies at the same time; I had to deal with the clear and present danger that was drug addiction. Nothing else would get fixed without first sorting this. I knew I had to walk a tightrope in recovery. I also knew that some spiritual awakening had happened. Something just gave inside me and I knew I had to grab this chance with everything I had. Four days' detoxing without any substances. It was erratic. I didn't care. I knew I was getting better minute by minute. On the fifth day, I stopped smoking cigarettes. I thought, sod it; I don't want no damaging chemicals inside my head. I knew the PTSD and psychosis could flare up and I wanted to begin to rebalance everything and give my body, mind and spirit the best chance of healing.

One week clean and I cut out caffeine and sugar. During the day, I would be researching all forms of information on diet and so on. What would work to retrain the brain. I found out that 2 per cent of our decisions are made consciously and 94 to 96 per cent take place subconsciously. That's why advertising is aimed at the subconscious mind. I also found out that the subconscious mind cannot discern what is real or not. Hence when you have nightmares and flashbacks about ordeals in the past, to your body and mind it is real: you're full of adrenaline and other chemicals, sweating and so on. I knew I was sweating from the detoxing and the nightmares and my mind was in a poor state from sleep deprivation, but I had faith and belief that with an uber-strict rehabilitation programme I would make it out. One week turned into two weeks. Now I was attending meetings twice daily. I would do one to two hours guided meditation for various things like letting go of thoughts, to quieten the over-thinking and anxiety. Basically, it was just what a shrink would do but it was only me laid out on the sofa listening to YouTube. Same message, just a different delivery system. I made it to a month clean.

I felt a little more stable so I contacted my GP and asked for a referral for my non-visible injuries. I knew they would prescribe strong medication again. I was scared my addiction would take over. For me, I knew that taking substances to escape the reality of the situation could migrate to the misuse of prescribed medication; in fact, it was easier to justify as these were from a health professional and you were taking action to assist your recovery. Still, the danger is the same. You build up a tolerance and want more and more to get the same effect; it's a vicious circle and you are still nowhere near to sorting the real issues but now have an additional problem to deal with: addiction to the medication. The incentive to tackle the non-visible injuries is lost as you won't tackle the non-visible injuries because that's where the supply of drugs can be accessed. However, I knew I needed to be responsible, to make contact with health professionals and seek their help through the process, but after what I'd been through it was difficult.

I saw a community mental health nurse first. I think it was her first experience of a war veteran. It was my first time with a health professional in a while. The anger inside me was brutal, not towards her but those that came before her. I knew this wasn't healthy. There had been delays in getting my medical records and I thought here we go again. I was booked in to see the psychiatrist the following week or so. The NHS is stretched and the process was slow, but I said to myself I'm not going back to where I've been; I'm six weeks clean and I'm making progress. Whatever it would take I was going to bloody mend by any means possible. The quack asked the usual bullshit questions. I really didn't want to be there. The anger was seething, but that was just from all the past experience. I had no animosity towards these people. I just didn't trust the system. I went straight to the pharmacy to get my medication. At home, I sat and stared at the box of very strong tablets; I knew what they were like, what effect they would have on me.

I took one out of the packet and I remembered the last time, sitting on the sofa dribbling, slowly dying inside. I put it back in the wrapper and placed the medication in the drawer. I made the decision to do this without medication. I knew I would only abuse the medication so early on in addiction recovery. I really didn't want any mood-altering substances or chemicals affecting my mind. I had had a lifetime's worth of that shit. I had the determination and belief that recovery could and would be done without chemicals. I was only going to be taking the medication prescribed by the doctor for a few months and then they would assess if I was ready for therapy. If not, more pills, more ills. I thought fuck this, I'm going to make it and show them all I can do this for myself.

I made it ten weeks clean and visited the psychiatrist again. I owned up to the fact that I hadn't taken the medication; I couldn't lie to them. I just was completely honest. I brought in the medication and showed her none had been consumed and I didn't want it. I had calmed down a lot and she did note this. I also had a stable regime of exercise, good diet, meditation and guided meditation. I knew the only person who was going to fix me was me. There was no way they could talk me into anything, not after what had happened with the treatment at Combat Stress. The private consultant I had been seeing who had diagnosed me with the nervous breakdown, on top of everything else, concluded that I was immune to treatment; the effect of the mistreatment at Combat Stress and by the MOD. I would not be able to be talked round into believing anything that came out of their mouths and he was right. He was pushing for me to get electroconvulsive therapy (ECT), which is basically electric shocks delivered to trigger a seizure. There would be a good chance that it would wipe my memory. I had plenty of good memories and the bad ones were acceptable so I wanted to keep the good ones. So I had nothing to lose. I told the shrink that I was on a spiritual path and it was like an awakening, and after years of hardship things were moving in the right direction. Talking about that to a psychiatrist is like recommending the competition. I even joked with her that she could do with an invisible friend in her life. Oh, her pen was going crazy taking notes. I just laughed. Sod it, I deserved to smile.

She said she would be in contact to arrange another appointment. I was open to anything; life was looking up. Positive things were starting to happen. I mean I didn't watch television either. I had nothing going into my body apart from recovery in some form or another. I became partly vegetarian, eating only fish and dairy products. You name it, I would try it to see if it would help. If it did, I stuck with it. If it didn't, I dropped it. I was working on my recovery from addiction and on recovery from war. I felt strong even though it was now coming up to three months of being clean. I had been giving this a lot of thought during this time. How come it worked this time and what had changed? I know I had been dreaming of getting better and putting real emotion into that. I knew the one thing that had driven me even during the darkest days was that I would get better so I could help others or at least right the wrong of the way veterans were being treated. I decided that I was going to write down my story and where and what I had been through to inspire others and also to shed some light on what is happening to veterans with non-visible injuries; make the public more aware. It would be part of my treatment. It's just what you would do with a therapist anyway, so why not do my recovery through a book and show others it can be done if you really want to do it?

I started writing this book when I was ninety days clean. So here I was in treatment for addiction, trying alternative and standard treatments for non-visible injuries, making my own way and I thought, I know; why don't I just add writing a memoir to it? I know it may sound crazy but I knew it was what I should do. It's hard to explain but I felt, and I still do, that everything I had endured was for a reason and that reason was that I could make a difference to others going through the recovery from non-visible injuries or whatever has caused you suffering in your life. I used to be first in the door or lead scout in my patrol in war. This is no different: I was taking the fight to the enemy in my mind, leading the way and inspiring others.

If I can do it then there is no reason others can't. There are many, many people that have to deal with addiction and non-visible injuries who, for them too, medication is not the option. I chose a spiritual and holistic path and believe that nothing compares to it. To know you can get through anything, it's just about breaking down that initial door. Knowing where to start and that there is peace, even joy, on the other side. The negativity of illness keeps you down, but if you start dreaming and see yourself as better in the future that's the start. It may take quite some time or it may be quick, but you have got to see yourself on the other side of this. That's why I've always called it a non-visible injury; it's the mindset. You can't see it and an injury is only temporary. I knew it was only temporary. It was hell on earth but I had faith in myself. Time after time. Fall after fall. Recall what I swore before God in that meeting with Combat Stress: 'I have seen too many good men blown to bits or shot to shit to roll over and play dead', and so have you. You have not gone through whatever trauma in your life just to be a victim. Make a firm decision: no matter how goddam hard it gets, no matter how tough it becomes, I'm bloody well going to make it. Don't ever stop saying it until it happens.

In my early recovery, I attended a day-care centre to get me out of isolation; it was uncomfortable and a lot of the time I didn't want to be there but I persevered with it. I knew it would be beneficial. I was willing to try it. My mind started to open. I would see solutions, not problems. Initially I was a critic, even of myself, but with time the doubt goes away. I was introduced to reflexology. The lady, Tina, who started working with me when I was only two weeks into my self-treatment, opened up the energy to start healing myself. It was one tool I used. I use many, many tools; whatever works. I got creative about what I needed to do and how to do it. I stumbled across a book by Bob Proctor, *The Art of Living*. It explains a little about the universal laws that govern everything we do. I started studying these laws so as to practise them in my day-to-day life. It is an ongoing process, but they are paying dividends already.

I hadn't the first clue about how to write a book but I knew I would do it. That's where everything starts. It starts with a decision. Once you get that desire entrenched into your mind you start to open up to ways and means of bringing that desire into reality. A lot of the stuff I was studying I had been doing already throughout my life. I just focused my energy. I disciplined my emotions. I wanted to write so I placed myself around writers, joined a writers' circle, visited writing events and libraries, just to immerse myself in the craft. I purchased a simple book titled *How to Write a Book ASAP*, that was the main mentor for me in achieving this. I followed the instructions step by step. Like my recovery and treatment, step by step, day by day. It's good to look at the whole picture. Yes, picture yourself at your destination or whatever task or goal you want to achieve and then instead of the usual question, 'Can I do this?', reframe your thoughts. Anyone can do it. It is more a question of 'Do you want to do it?' If so, then ask yourself, 'How do I do this?'

You start at the finish line and then work back to where you are now. Then there you have it: a step-by-step plan on how to achieve your goal. Then you make it into the only thing you desire. It will build and when you keep working on it, keep pushing through the barriers and hardships, doors open, things come to you out of the blue. It is truly that simple. Just believe it, see it, feel yourself in the place you want to be and it will manifest, but you must be disciplined, precise and relentless. I commenced studying about living in the now, not what we all do in either living in the past or the future but in the here and now. I studied Eckhart Tolle's *The Power of Now*. There is an abundance of messages and literature out there for you, if you're ready for it. Make no mistake, nothing will be revealed to you that you're not ready for.

For veterans or anyone else who needs to heal, anyone who has had their peace stolen from them and had it replaced with a war inside your head, the most important thing I learned and continue to learn in recovery and try to practise is to find other veterans or people with whom you can identify and with whom you have a common bond. Listen and learn from them. Share your story: what you did to get you through; what works for you. When you share your peace with others, you will receive it back in bucketloads. I feel I am truly blessed to have gone through all of that so I can help others with it. People can identify with what I've been through and when I talk to people they are open-minded to my suggestions. That's a great gift. To help save people's lives. I struggled deeply with that aspect of war for quite some time. During my time in war I had heard other lads on about my kill count and so on. In the end, I stopped counting; I knew it would be a bittersweet pill.

There are many aspects of war with which we all must make peace. When you change your outlook and start to rationalize it in a positive manner, the one great emotion is gratitude. I started feeling gratitude for being alive and wanting to be alive. Gratitude for my recovery and gratitude for being able to help others in recovery. I reached out to veterans' charities to give back and continue to do so. I reached out to people suffering from addiction to give something back and continue to do so. I will continue to give back to those that need it. My life is amazing. For too long I thought I had lost it all. That life was unfair. I was full of guilt and shame about being ill and the mistreatment I suffered, blaming everybody and everything for where I was in my life, but I do not give myself a hard time about it and nor should you. When you are in negativity you draw more of that in and it is difficult to break out, but you can do it in small steps. You will probably fail many times but that is where the growth is at. That is where your pain will drive you onwards to change. I embraced my pain; it drove me onwards at the start for all the wrong reasons but you can only work with the tools you have. As I progressed and started to realize that it is an inner journey, that's what life is about, it is about being inner-directed, not letting whatever your present circumstances are get to you. Start to concentrate on working on yourself from the inside out and in no time the outside changes automatically, but with as anything new it takes repetitive practice. Like any skill it is through constant perseverance that it becomes second nature; it must be ingrained in your subconscious mind for it to take effect, so I knew I had to try to let go of the past.

What's done is done. I've moved on now. In life, everyone plays their part; even those who do wrong have their part to play. I don't hold any grudge against any institution or agency because I know it's not the ideas or institutions that are the issue, it's the people within them. Not all but quite a few, and they need to be held accountable in a fair and democratic society. We went to war to uphold values like this. I'm certainly not going to abandon them when one feels the need for revenge. That anger, pain and resentment against those who have wronged or harmed you, it only grows darker and darker inside you until you're a sheer burning hell of torment; you may not be ready yet but even knowing you will do what I did will help in the long run. I forgave those who had wronged me. I let go to grow; not for them but for my peace, my mind, my soul. Don't fret if that is absolutely the last thing you want to do with anyone yet. Hey, my friend, I would have skinned them alive, boiled them and watched while eating popcorn, so I understand. Yet in the end it won't do you any good; it will only cause you harm and you will live in the torment for longer. When you're ready it will pass, my friend.

Now I see all that as a huge gift. I am humbled by my experience and because of that experience I can now save lives, not take lives. Because of that gift, I can overcome anything, anywhere, anytime. I got back my faith in myself and in others and in everything. I am unbreakable. I am unstoppable. Just think for a minute, my friend, when in your life did you decide to become a victim? When did you decide that you would let everything beat you? When did you decide you don't want to do anything? It's up to you what you want to do. There is nothing different about any of us. The only difference is our mindset.

To veterans I say this: yes, war can be shit at times but it can also be a wonderful place. Remember those acts of courage, of kindness, acts of camaraderie. I've seen the very worst of what we humans can do, but I've also witnessed the very best. There was no charity, no politician, no banker, nobody but us on the battlefield. We didn't think about them or need them when it was our time to stand. We certainly don't need to rely on them entirely now.

Yes, access those services to get treatment or for whatever reason, but nobody is going to fix you. It's you who fixes you. Stop thinking of this post-traumatic stress. I think, therefore I am. Yes, we have been through trauma but I'm not going to let this keep me down. I'm not going to let this ruin my life. I'm not going to play the same shit over and over again any more. I'm coming back. I'm going to be better. I'm going to heal myself. I'm going to be stronger as a result of this, not weaker. The two most important words you will ever know are I AM. What you put after I AM is up to you. I am a veteran. Okay, that's fine, so what are you going to do? Yes, we are veterans but that's a part of us, not all of us. What are you going to be after you come home from war, once you free yourself from the war in your mind? The writer Mark Twain quoted: 'The two most important days in your life are the day you are born and the day you find out why.' Most people on the planet never ask why they are here, so here I will do it for you. Why are you here? It is a simple question, but boy does it resonate with you. Please keep looking for the answer until you find it and once you do, go after it. The bottom of the heap of life is full of people who don't want to empower themselves, waiting for someone or something to save them. Look at nature; does anything in nature wait to be saved? No, it does what it can in preparing and evolving. If it does not, it withers, dies and is cast away in the ground to be reused by something else. Life is fair: if you put bugger all in, you will get bugger all out.

For those still in the trenches, all I can say is this: I was there, my friend. It is getting better. While there is breath in your body, you're still in the fight. You may have been knocked down, but you ain't knocked out. Many of us have been where you are right now. There is a way out and it starts with accepting your situation and then doing something about it. Keep telling yourself, I am going to make it, because sooner or later you will if you just have belief in yourself. Finally, help end the bullshit. Once you have healed yourself, get out and help others and pass on the message of recovery. Also, let's begin to call this illness non-visible injury. It's all in the mindset. Change your life. Change your world. Change your mind. Turn Trauma into Triumph.

Afterword

Ask yourself the following questions. If the answers are yes, I hope the subsequent advice/suggestions may be of help to you:

- Are you self-medicating on drink/drugs?
- Do you think you have a problem with drink/drugs?

It may be difficult for you to tell anyone about your situation, but speaking to your GP would really be a positive step for you. If you can do this, try to be as honest as you can; it will help you more in the long term. Asking for help is one of the most courageous acts you can do for yourself.

If you want to try other routes before speaking to your GP, you can search for alcohol and drug services in your area; they can be a one-stop shop for recovery from alcohol and drug problems. Many will be able to point you in the right direction for assistance with your non-visible injuries. If you do not want to disclose that, it's okay; getting off the drink and drugs is a huge personal step in your fight back to health. I can guarantee that by sorting these issues or at least taking steps in the right direction it will benefit you.

There are also mutual aid groups. These are groups usually put together by others in recovery, like the twelve-step programme where like-minded people help each other in the process of recovery. There are plenty out there. Start searching online for what is near to you.

There are also many veterans' groups/charities that can assist you in your area:

- The Royal British Legion: http://www.britishlegion.org.uk
- SSAFA: https://www.ssafa.org.uk

These two have stood the test of time and are good anchor-points for gaining more access to more services. If you are unable to leave the house but you have internet access, it may be slower but at least it will be a starting-point. Search for online recovery sites; there are literally thousands worldwide and some are even veteran-specific. Get in contact. You can chat over Skype and so on to like-minded people. You will start to mend. These are all positive steps.

Try to aim to leave the house once a day, even if it's only to the end of the street or to a local park. Get into nature; even staring at dogs running around in the park works wonders.

This all takes time but admitting to yourself that you need help is the biggest step. So well done for being honest and courageous with yourself and give yourself a break. You're injured. It is perfectly natural to feel how you feel. Sod everybody else. This is about you and saving your life. If you are not ready for this at the moment, then that's cool too.

If you're still at the height of the drink and drugs phase, well if I said stop, would you? I didn't. So let's use the tools that you have, that is, the drink and drugs. You're going to be in some fantasy land while consuming them before the paranoia sets in, so turn it to your advantage. Start dreaming that you're going to get better and get off the drink and drugs, even if you're going to do it to become a porn star; just go with it. Start seeing yourself on the other side of recovery, looking healthy, fitter and so on. It's your dream, so dream big. Visualize yourself after treatment. Feel how good that feels. Work with it. Try positive meditation on YouTube. Do some every day. It doesn't happen overnight but keep going. See your life after getting help. Picture all the good things. It doesn't matter if you're Napoleon on the sofa; it all begins with a thought. I think, therefore I am.

Index